D0066734

THE
CREDEAUX
CANVAS

BY KEITH BUNIN

★

★

DRAMATISTS
PLAY SERVICE
INC.

THE CREDEAUX CANVAS
Copyright © 2002, Keith Bunin

All Rights Reserved

SPECIAL NOTE

for my parents and sister

THE CREDEAUX CANVAS was produced by Playwrights Horizons (Tim Sanford, Artistic Director; Leslie Marcus, Managing Director; William Russo, General Manager) in New York City on May 11, 2001. It was directed by Michael Mayer; the set design was by Derek McLane; the lighting design was by Kenneth Posner; the sound design was by Scott Myers; the costume design was by Michael Krass; the fight director was J. Steven White; the production manager was Christopher Boll; and the production stage manager was J. Philip Bassett. The cast was as follows:

AMELIA .... Annie Parisse
WINSTON .... Lee Pace
JAMIE .... Glenn Howerton
TESS .... E. Katherine Kerr

CHARACTERS

AMELIA

WINSTON

JAMIE

TESS

PLACE

An attic apartment on East 10th Street in New York City.

TIME

The present.

SCENE BREAKDOWN

Act One

Scene 1: A Tuesday morning in early March.
Scene 2: 11:30 that Saturday night.

Act Two

Scene 1: 3 P.M. on a Thursday in April.
Scene 2: Dusk on a Sunday in October, four years later.

THE CREDEAUX CANVAS

ACT ONE

Scene 1

An attic apartment on East 10th Street in New York City. A chilly Tuesday morning in early March.

A skylight with mismatched panes of glass. Flaking paint and chipped drywall but lovely prewar detail: hardwood floors and window seats.

A heavy-looking door leads to the hallway and a flimsy-looking door leads to the bathroom. Hanging from the open portal that leads to the bedroom are floor-to-ceiling beads which obscure our view.

A kitchen counter with a few grimy cabinets. A scary old oven. A half-sized refrigerator. No sink.

A narrow mattress along one wall. A work table littered with paints, brushes, sketch pads, and canvases.

In the center of the room is an easel. On the easel is a canvas. The canvas faces away from us, as it always will.

Amelia, 20s, stands just behind the easel. She is dressed in a man's plaid bathrobe. She is sweet and gregarious and East Village chic. She stares raptly at the canvas.

Winston, 20s, rolls over in bed and rubs the sleep from his eyes. He wears an old T-shirt and paint-spattered sweatpants. He is gangly and hesitant but deeply fervent. He considers Amelia very closely before he decides to speak.

WINSTON. It's a fake.

AMELIA. *(Startled and caught.)* I didn't mean to pry.

WINSTON. Not really a fake, it's just not, you know, *mine.*

AMELIA. It isn't?

WINSTON. *(Tremendously self-effacing.)* It's an assignment for school, it's too complicated to explain, and you wouldn't be interested anyway.

AMELIA. No, no, I *am* interested. See, sometimes I wake up in the middle of the night, and I hear you out here, faintly, your brush scraping against the canvas. *(Winston takes out a box of cereal from beneath his blankets and eats as he watches Amelia talk.)* So I've always wanted to come out here and *talk* to you, I've been dating Jamie for six *months* now, can you *believe* it, I sleep over here practically every *night,* but I've barely exchanged two *words* with you.

WINSTON. I know, it's ridiculous, isn't it?

AMELIA. Well, here's our chance.

WINSTON. Yeah, um, here's our chance. *(They subside into a silence that is at first expectant and then deeply uncomfortable. Finally Amelia gestures to the canvas.)*

AMELIA. Well. I really like your painting. I do.

WINSTON. Oh. Um. Thanks. But. Like I said. It's a forgery.

AMELIA. A forgery?

WINSTON. A school assignment. You take, um, a painting you admire and, uh, you copy it.

AMELIA. Why would you do that? *(Winston steps a little closer to both Amelia and the easel.)*

WINSTON. The point, um, is to study the techniques and the grammar of another painter in such a way as to maybe, you know, hopefully *internalize* the process of a master artist. Because then, you can, I guess, not only appropriate some new and useful tools but you can also shed some light on your own grammar and techniques, I think, learn how to articulate and master your own talents.

AMELIA. *(Very brightly.)* I don't understand a single word you just said.

WINSTON. *(Flushes bright red.)* Now, see, people always try to draw me out. But once I start talking, you know, pretty quickly everyone wants me to shut up again.

AMELIA. I don't want that. *(He goes to the table, picks up an open book, and holds it out to her.)*

WINSTON. Oh. Okay. Here's, um, a reproduction of the original painting.

AMELIA. *(Takes the book from him.)* I've never seen this before.

WINSTON. It's kind of, you know, obscure. I saw the actual painting last summer, in this tiny museum just outside Paris.

AMELIA. I've never been to France.

WINSTON. *(Getting very excited.)* Neither had I. I felt totally compelled to go, I mean, the Fauvists were my first obsession, and there were so many paintings I loved that I'd only seen in books. In a way it was a really self-destructive thing to do, I spent literally my last dime on the trip, I've been subsisting on ramen noodles and tap water all semester, but, um, it was definitely worth it, to discover this.

AMELIA. Who painted it?

WINSTON. Jean-Paul Credeaux. You've never heard of him. He's practically unknown.

AMELIA. *(Impressed.)* So this totally is your discovery.

WINSTON. *(Stuffs his hands in his pockets.)* I guess. He's really, um, a complete anomaly. Not really a Fauvist and not really a Post-Impressionist. But he borrowed, um, liberally from both camps, and he managed to fuse these disparate influences together in a way that was also somehow entirely classical and representational. You don't care about any of this.

AMELIA. *(Smiles pleasantly at him.)* Not really, but I like hearing you talk about it.

WINSTON. *(Plowing right on.)* I get obsessed with certain painters. Last year it was Helen Frankenthaler. This great Abstract Expressionist. For a whole semester everything I painted looked like her masterpiece, this amazing painting called *Mountains and Sea.*

AMELIA. *(Hands the book back to him.)* Well, this really is a wonderful painting. *(Winston takes the book from her and puts it on the*

9

table, chattering all the way, completely lit up.)

WINSTON. Technically there's nothing like it. It's as casual as a watercolor but he's working in oils so he's got depth of color and tonal control as well. And the brushwork is so economical: It almost feels like he's afraid he's about to run out of paint. Yet it doesn't seem the least bit over-thought. It retains the freshness and discovery of, um, a preliminary sketch. *(He heads back toward her, his arms gesticulating with wild excitement. She watches him very closely.)*

AMELIA. I can't believe nobody knows about him.

WINSTON. That's all going to change very soon. Mark my words, five years from now there'll be a major exhibit of Jean-Paul Credeaux's paintings here in New York, and the lines will stretch around the block. See, everyone used to think that all he left behind were these still lifes. Expertly well-crafted, you know, and gorgeous, but in a lot of people's minds essentially inconsequential.

AMELIA. *(With a jovial conviviality.)* What do they know, right?

WINSTON. But just recently it's become apparent that during the last years of his life he completed an entirely different set of paintings. He painted them, um, under a bunch of pseudonyms, so they've been almost impossible to trace. But, um, two of them have just been officially attributed to him. There are definitely at least five more. Probably there are a few others that have been destroyed.

AMELIA. Destroyed? Why?

WINSTON. The thing is, the people he sold them to, they weren't exactly connoisseurs of fine art. In fact, to be precise, the paintings weren't actually *sold* at all. They were more like *bartered*. He'd give them away to cover his gambling debts. Apparently he was really lousy at cards.

AMELIA. That's kind of sweet, to think that a bunch of loan sharks would be mollified by a few paintings.

WINSTON. I don't think they were all that interested in paintings per se. What they were really interested in was, um, the *subjects* of these particular paintings. These happen to be, you see, a series of, um, nude portraits of, you know, prostitutes.

AMELIA. Aha.

WINSTON. Solely intended to be viewed in the seclusion of a gentleman's private quarters.

AMELIA. Sort of a rarefied kind of centerfold, then.

10

WINSTON.   Right. Except these, ironically, happen to be, um, brilliant.

AMELIA.   You've seen them?

WINSTON.   *(Getting very excited again.)* Only the two that have been officially attributed. And only reproductions. In an article. Which I have here somewhere. *(Quickly he starts rummaging through the books and papers on his table.)* It's the, um, extraordinary quality of the light, you can see it even in the photographs. *(He finds the magazine and starts riffling through the pages.)* And somehow he doesn't even seem to be painting the women. It seems like he just, um, paints the sunlight that's shining on them, and the women, you know, are just *there*, revealed by the light. *(He finds the right page and thrusts the magazine toward Amelia. She takes it from him and considers the pictures, a little confused.)*

AMELIA.   I can sort of see what you mean, I guess. *(Excitedly, he comes very close to her and points at the pictures in the magazine.)*

WINSTON.   And there's this, you know, amazing complicity between the painter and the subject. It's erotic, sure, but it's also deeply unsettling. Which isn't surprising, I guess, since six months after he finished these paintings he was dead from syphilis.

AMELIA.   Not a model citizen, your Credeaux.

WINSTON.   But, you know, a genius nonetheless. *(Amelia turns to look at him. Winston turns abruptly away.)* I don't mean to be rude, but, um, my shift at the library starts at noon, and really I ought to, you know, um.

AMELIA.   *(Puts her hand to her heart.)* Oh! Of course! You want to get some work done!

WINSTON.   If you don't mind.

AMELIA.   No, no, you've been way too indulgent of me. *(Winston pulls his chair over to the easel and starts setting up his paints and brushes.)*

WINSTON.   You can talk all you want, you won't distract me, but I do need to, you know, *work*, so if that's not too inconsiderate —

AMELIA.   Please, you've been nothing but a gracious host.

WINSTON.   Plus actually I *like* being distracted. Generally I'm way too obsessive.

AMELIA.   *(Riding him a little.)* Really.

WINSTON.   *(Smiles sheepishly at her.)* So, um, I appreciate all the distractions I get. *(Gestures to the canvas.)* *This* is actually kind of a distraction. It's a piddly little assignment for one of my electives. *(He extends his arm to indicate the canvases that sit on the work table propped up against the wall.)* That's what I really should be working on. My own stuff, for my master's thesis. But I avoid working by working, so I sit here all morning, copying out a Credeaux canvas. *(He goes to work. Amelia sits at the kitchen table and watches him.)*

AMELIA. I'm just gonna sit here quiet as a mouse till Jamie gets back.

WINSTON. Yeah, what sprung him out of bed at the crack of dawn?

AMELIA. *(Consults her watch.)* At the moment, he should be showing an apartment on West End Avenue. But eight o'clock this morning was the reading of his father's will.

WINSTON. Gosh, whoa, I forgot that was today.

AMELIA. *(Biting at her nails.)* I hope it went well for him. I hope his father had one of those deathbed conversions you hear so much about. Realized what a shit he'd been to Jamie all his life, felt so guilty about it that he left Jamie every penny.

WINSTON. That, you know, that would be terrific.

AMELIA. I mean, I never met the man, but to hear the stories, he sounds like a bastard. *(Winston is working steadily. Amelia sits there watching him.)*

WINSTON. He was, I guess, pretty much a bastard. He had one talent, which was that he could walk into a room full of people and somehow immediately sense the disbursement of power among them. Who to suck up to, who to insult, who to completely ignore. All, you know, so he could amass the largest amount of power for himself.

AMELIA. Sounds like a real joy to be around.

WINSTON. In my opinion that's the only reason he was such a successful art dealer. From my few conversations with him it was clear he didn't have a shred of taste himself.

AMELIA. You've got to feel awful for Jamie, growing up in that house.

WINSTON. *(Shaking his head.)* The byzantine tortures his dad inflicted on him. One time I was over at the house, um, for absolutely no reason, all through dinner the guy was flicking peas at the back of Jamie's head. If I had to live with that man for eighteen years, I swear to God, I would've swallowed a bottle of pills, too.

AMELIA. *(Pricking up her ears.)* So you were around for all that?

WINSTON. *(Nods, looks down.)* His dad signed the commitment papers and went right back to his office. He didn't visit the whole time Jamie was in the hospital.

AMELIA. You've known Jamie a long time, then.

WINSTON. We were roommates my first semester undergraduate.

AMELIA. I always forget Jamie went to art school.

WINSTON. *(With a laugh.)* I'm sure he'd like to forget it himself. It was a colossal error. He was on one of his kamikaze missions for his father's approval, so out of the blue he decided he was a painter. I don't even know how he got *in*. He didn't have a portfolio. He must've conned and flirted his way through the entire admissions department.

AMELIA. *(Good-humored.)* He's terrific at conning and flirting, I can tell you *that*.

WINSTON. He spent the whole semester working on this truly bizarre mural kind of thing. It was part representational and part abstract and all butt-ugly. Our instructor wouldn't even grade it. Jamie dropped out the next day.

AMELIA. Poor guy.

WINSTON. Lucky, in a way, that he found out so quickly it wasn't what he was supposed to be doing.

AMELIA. Well. It's a rare thing to know what you're supposed to be doing. You're really fortunate, you know that.

WINSTON. You too. I mean, I hear you're a wonderful singer.

AMELIA. *(Turning bright red.)* Oh, please.

WINSTON. Jamie always, um, invites me to your gigs, and I always intend to go, truly, it's just that whenever I have a free moment I feel totally compelled to, you know, *work*.

AMELIA. Don't be silly, I completely understand. Almost nobody shows up anymore anyway. It seems like we're playing later and later at night in more and more dangerous neighborhoods.

WINSTON. Well, to hear Jamie tell it, you're destined for greatness.

AMELIA. Jamie comes to every show and sits right next to the stage and whoops like an orangutan after every song.

WINSTON. *(With a laugh.)* Jamie thinks I'm brilliant too. He was sure his father would take one look at my stuff and, you know, he'd immediately want to sign me up, and I'd be an instant millionaire. So we carted a bunch of paintings up to the house, his dad looked at them and just laughed, he said, "Check back with me in five years."

AMELIA. What a prick.

WINSTON. *(Shrugs his shoulders.)* Actually I thought it was a pretty fair assessment of my accomplishments at the time. Check back in five years. *(A beat.)* You've always wanted to be a singer, huh?

AMELIA. *(Very lightly.)* Sure. But I'm a quarter of a century old now, and I haven't earned a dime at it. What I really am is a waitress. Except last week I got fired from Miracle Grill for calling in sick too many shifts, so now I'm something even worse which is an *unemployed* waitress.

WINSTON. I'm, you know, a really bad library checkout clerk. And I'll tell you, it takes tremendous ineptitude of some kind to be a really bad library checkout clerk.

AMELIA. I circle ads in the *Village Voice*, and then I go out to apply for a job which if I get I know I'll hate. And which I never get anyway. I had this interview yesterday at the Cornelia Street Café, the manager lady gave me a written exam. To be a *waitress! (The sound of heavy footsteps coming up the stairs. Winston pricks up his ears in anticipation.)* And the first question was, "In an ideal world, the dessert fork would be in what relation to the plate?" I wanted to say, lady, in an ideal world I would never have to lay *eyes* on you.

WINSTON. There's Jamie on the stairs.

AMELIA. When I was growing up in Ridgefield, all I ever thought about was coming to New York to be a singer. And now I'm here and all I ever think about is money. *(The door is flung open, and Jamie, 20s, stands beneath the transom. His hair is slicked back, and he is dressed very sharply in an overcoat and suit. He is a deeply charismatic and infectiously enthusiastic young man. In his hands he carries two large shopping bags. He extends his arms to Winston and Amelia.)*

JAMIE. In years to come, tales of my unparalleled munificence will spread far and wide throughout the land. Epic poems will be written, ballads will be composed, all entirely in my honor. *(Jamie drops his shopping bags on the floor, goes to Amelia, kisses her deeply on the mouth, and wraps his arms around her tightly.)* And in these ballads they will sing of you, the siren, the nymph, whose breath-taking voice is so glorious it can launch ships, it can melt glaciers, it makes any man who hears her fall to his knees in wonder.

AMELIA. Now I'm blushing. *(Jamie steps out of the embrace and moves to Winston at the easel. He puts one arm around Winston's neck and rubs Winston's scalp with his knuckles.)*

JAMIE. And they will sing of my loyal compatriot, the genius who paints with fire on the tip of his brush, who toiled away in patient obscurity until the masses were finally ready to receive his greatness, and then he descended the mountain to the deafening cheers of the entire populace.

WINSTON. *(Blushing a little himself.)* Wow, um, that's quite a, wow. *(Jamie extracts food from the shopping bags with the flair of a magician performing a particularly elaborate trick.)*

JAMIE. Behold the bounty I have brought you. I give you muffins, I give you croissants, I give you scones for pete's sake. Plus the most baroque varieties of cappuccinos and lattés. And I am here to tell you that after today we will never go hungry again. *(Winston and Amelia stare at him, their arms and mouths overstuffed with various pastries and coffees.)*

WINSTON. So, um, I guess it went well at the lawyer's, huh? *(Jamie grins, pulls off his overcoat and drapes it over a chair.)*

JAMIE. It was remarkable. It was transcendent. It was an hon-est-to-God religious experience.

AMELIA. *(Her mouth full of scone.)* The old man on his deathbed comes through. How about that?

JAMIE. *(Rubbing his hands together.)* So I walk out of the wood-paneled elevator into the wood-paneled office past the wood-paneled secretary, and I brazenly take a seat right next to Gail, my stepmother, remember her, with the hair? *(Winston and Amelia nod eagerly.)* Who looked absolutely shocked to see me, but I could be wrong about that, she's had so many facelifts, it's possible that these days she just looks shocked all the time. *(Winston starts putting his paints away, still listening intently.)* And she's brought her boys with her, those two little towheaded monsters, and they're climbing all over the wing-back chairs, literally gnawing off huge chunks of the upholstery. Plus there are any number of goons representing an endless parade of hearse-chasing foundations and trusts.

WINSTON. *(Not impatient, just anxious.)* So, Jamie, how much, you know, did you get?

JAMIE. *(Raises his arms.)* My father's lawyer, Claude, he's a hundred years old so it takes him forever to list all the beneficiaries: Gail, the little blond children of the damned, the Whitney, the Guggenheim, the Audubon Society, maybe even the Daughters of the American Revolution, I'm not sure, I dozed off for a second. Then he closes his ledger. *(Smiles darkly at them.)* And my name was not even mentioned.

AMELIA. *(In a low voice.)* This is very bad.

JAMIE. *(Reveling in the humiliation.)* As if I had been completely erased from his memory, as if I never even *existed*.

WINSTON. But, um, I don't understand, why did they tell you to come if you weren't going to get anything?

JAMIE. At the end of it, I went up to Claude, and I asked him, why am I even here? *(Winston and Amelia nod, watching him with a growing concern.)* And he said, "Frankly, Jamie, I think it's horrible your father did this, and I wanted you to know about it because, off the record, if you contested the will I think you might have a case."

AMELIA. *(Immediately worried.)* You're not going to try and do that, are you?

JAMIE. *(With a laugh.)* Sure, I'll hire a lawyer, since I have so much cash to burn. I'll argue my case in an endless succession of courts till I'm old and grey, finally maybe I'll wrest a picayune chunk of change away from Gail and her little brats. Thanks but no thanks.

AMELIA. Well, that seems like the most mature —

JAMIE. *(Riding over her.)* So then I have to dash over to West End Avenue to show this absurdly sumptuous triplex to this unbearably drippy couple just in from Raleigh, they're exactly our age, and they're worth six hundred eighty-four million dollars, apparently he invented *software*. And the place is mouthwatering but she's upset because the columns are doric instead of ionic, and he can't figure out where he'd put his pool table.

WINSTON. *(Lightly ironic.)* Sure, well, everyone has a cross to bear.

JAMIE. *(Extends his arms to the apartment.)* And I wanted to scream at them, I don't have a kitchen *sink*, I wash my dishes in the *bathtub*, I eat one meal a day if I'm *lucky*, I treat myself so shabbily, I take much better care of this *suit*.

AMELIA. *(Intensely placating.)* You should quit that real-estate job, it only makes you miserable.

JAMIE. *(Letting his rage out now.)* I mean, I was *born* in this city. This is my *home*. But I can barely afford to *live* here. I break my back at these soul-sucking jobs, and for what? To meet the rent on this rat-infested *box* on this crummy *block* where every day I can wave hello to the friendly crack dealer on the corner?

AMELIA. Janelle's going out of town, you can pick up her shifts at the bar.

JAMIE. So I'm stumbling down West End Avenue, and who do I happen to run into walking her bichon friese but Tess Anderson Rose. *(Jamie makes a punctuating gesture. Winston and Amelia stare blankly.)*

WINSTON. I'm, uh, not sure, should I know who that is?

JAMIE. She was my father's prize client, she bought gazillions of dollars worth of paintings from him, and she's also, not incidentally, a prize ninny, really, stupid as a stone.

AMELIA. *(Hand to her heart.)* This day just gets worse and worse.

JAMIE. And she gives me this big hug, and she starts yammering on about how much she misses my father, she's searched far and wide but she hasn't been able to find a dealer who's so empathetic to her tastes, who helps her anticipate the market, who can lead her to new discoveries.

WINSTON. Okay, so, at this point, you're in the ninth circle of hell.

JAMIE. *(Raises his hands in the air.)* And all of a sudden straight from the heavens a thunderbolt of inspiration strikes directly at my brain. It is, I swear to God, the greatest piece of brilliance since the dawn of time.

WINSTON. *(With a laugh.)* We're allowing, I guess, for a certain amount of hyperbole here.

JAMIE. I told her I have a Credeaux. *(Jamie extends his arms in triumph. Winston and Amelia stare at him, completely dumbfounded.)*

AMELIA. I don't understand.

JAMIE. *(With cheerful nonchalance.)* I explained to her that just before my father died, he gave me a few paintings from his private collection. He did it secretly, he didn't even tell his lawyer, because he didn't want Gail to know. And one of the paintings he gave me was a Jean-Paul Credeaux.

WINSTON. This is, wow, kind of pathological, isn't it?

JAMIE. It's a totally credible story.

AMELIA. It just happens to be entirely untrue.

JAMIE. *(Turns to Winston.)* Lucky for me you've been yammering on about that guy all month. I knew all the right things to say to her. Of course she knows exactly who he is. She even owns one of his paintings. And she reads those same art journals you do, she's the worst kind of pretentious poseur.

WINSTON. *(Good-humored.)* I'm not certain, but, um, I think I've just been insulted.

JAMIE. So she knows in a few years anything by Credeaux will be worth a fortune, you should've seen her beady eyes light up with greed.

AMELIA. But you don't have a Credeaux.

JAMIE. *(Holding Winston in his gaze.)* But I will soon, won't I? *(The light dawns. Winston and Amelia stare at Jamie, amazed.)*

WINSTON. Have you gone quietly out of your mind?

JAMIE. Negroponte says you're the best he's ever had in his class, right? And old lady Crosley, she hates everything you do, but even she says you're brilliant at copying other people's paintings.

WINSTON. That doesn't mean, you know, I'm good enough to commit fraud.

JAMIE. I have complete and utter faith in you. *(Amelia starts to laugh. Winston gestures toward the easel.)*

WINSTON. What, pretend this canvas is from 1902? It's got staples on the side, my name is written on the stretcher in magic marker —

JAMIE. We'll go to that antiques shop on Avenue B, we'll buy one of those old landscapes for twenty bucks and scrape it, those canvases date back to the turn of the century at least. And I'll sweet-talk Cynthia at my father's office, I'll get her to let me into the workroom, I'll steal an old frame —

AMELIA. *(Her laughter growing.)* This has got to be a joke.

WINSTON. *(Goes over to the work table.)* Plus, I mean, the paints I use, there are chemicals in these that weren't even invented when —

JAMIE. *(Riding over him.)* Oils are oils, they look the same as

18

they did a hundred years ago, you'd have to be an expert to tell the difference.

WINSTON. Right, well, all she has to do is call in an expert.

JAMIE. She's too vain. She thinks she's an expert herself. She's convinced she can spot a fake at twenty paces.

WINSTON. So, maybe she can.

JAMIE. *(Utterly triumphant.)* Half the stuff in her collection is fake. Practically everything she bought before she hooked up with my father. He tried to tell her once, but she wouldn't listen to him, she didn't want to know.

AMELIA. *(Through her laughter.)* I don't believe a single word you're saying.

WINSTON. You really think you can, um, pawn this off on her?

JAMIE. *(Shakes his head, grinning.)* No. Everyone says all the still lifes are accounted for, isn't that what you told me? You'd have to do an entirely new painting. One of the nudes. No one's sure what happened to some of them, right? No one even knows for certain how many of them there were.

WINSTON. *(Picks up the magazine from the table.)* But all I have to work from are these reproductions. And I'd have to use a completely different figure so it wouldn't be such an obvious forgery, so I'd either have to use a photo in a magazine or else I'd have to find a model who's completely trustworthy. *(Jamie triumphantly extends his arms toward Amelia. She stares at him and bursts into new laughter.)*

AMELIA. This conversation just gets more and more ridiculous.

JAMIE. *(Goes to her, very excited.)* Sweetie, all you have to do is pose for him. If any one of us isn't happy with the results we'll call the whole thing off.

AMELIA. You want me to take off my clothes for your room-mate?

JAMIE. Winston and I will be the only ones who'll ever know it was you. And it's for such a good cause.

AMELIA. *(Still laughing.)* Yeah, we're a gaggle of saints, bilking a helpless old lady out of her life savings.

JAMIE. She's far from helpless, and believe me it will be far from her life savings. No matter how big the check she writes it will not even be a drop in the bucket. *(Amelia's laughter slowly dies in her throat. She considers Jamie.)*

AMELIA. Are we really talking about this seriously here?

WINSTON. *(Laughs nervously.)* No. No.

JAMIE. *(Very firmly.)* If anything goes wrong I'll take full responsibility. I'll say you posed for a painting that Winston did for class and I squired it away for my own nefarious purposes.

AMELIA. This is insane.

JAMIE. *(Shaking his head.)* Actually it's the way I've been behaving up till this moment that's been crazy. Really, I'm injecting a necessary bit of rationality into the proceedings here. I know you both have been awfully concerned about me. And you have every right to be. *(Jamie leans in to them. They watch him very closely.)* I've been wandering around the city like a lost child. I sit in Barnes & Noble for hours on end and read stacks of magazines. I stand in the Virgin Mega Store listening to entire albums over and over. I've been nothing but a deficit of space.

WINSTON. Don't be, I mean, you're not.

JAMIE. But suddenly this morning it's crystal clear to me precisely how I should be spending my days. I should spend them helping you. I want to help the two of you.

AMELIA. *(Deeply touched.)* But you already *are* helping us.

JAMIE. I can't bear the thought of you hauling another tray of quesadillas over to a bunch of hedge-fund brokers from Hoboken. And I can't let you sit behind that library desk watching the seconds tick by. I know we've been proceeding under the rubric that talent will out, but I'm terrified you'll both work your fingers to the bone for years on end and nothing will ever happen.

AMELIA. That scares me too, believe me.

JAMIE. And I love the two of you more than anything else in this world. So it's my fondest desire to dedicate all my resources to being your guardian angel. And if we do this one thing — this one slightly risky but you have to admit courageous thing — there's a small chance we'll get in a little bit of trouble, but it's far more likely that there won't be any consequences at all. Except that we'll be free. *(Jamie stares at them, flush with passion and desperation. Amelia looks away. Winston stuffs his hands in his pockets.)*

WINSTON. I don't think I can, I mean, I'm not good enough to.

JAMIE. You're plenty good enough to do this. Screw what a bunch of old-fart professors say, screw what my father said, he never cared about paintings anyway, he only cared about the signatures. All I'm stealing is the signature. And because of the signature, people will actually look at the painting, and they'll see it's a masterpiece. And it *will* be a masterpiece because you painted it.

WINSTON. *(A moment, then.)* How much time would I have?

JAMIE. She's flying out tomorrow to visit her sister in Sedona. She won't be back till April.

WINSTON. *(Looks up at him.)* What the hell, right? *(Jamie goes to Winston and gives him a huge bear hug, lifting him several inches off the floor. Amelia watches mutely.)*

JAMIE. You are a great and true friend.

WINSTON. Well, I may go to jail for five years, but at least I'll ace my spring elective. *(Winston grabs his jeans from the bed and heads into the bathroom. Jamie dips into the shopping bag and pulls out a carton of juice.)*

JAMIE. Hey, hey, I bought orange juice, I thought we could make some screwdrivers to celebrate.

WINSTON. *(From the bathroom.)* I'm already fifteen minutes late for work, so why not? *(Jamie hauls down the vodka and two glasses from the cupboard.)*

JAMIE. *(Calls out to Winston.)* Could you get another clean glass from the tub?

WINSTON. *(From the bathroom.)* Sure. You know, actually my shift will probably go much faster if I'm tanked.

JAMIE. I'm dealing you in, too, honey. *(Jamie goes about fixing the screwdrivers. Changed into his jeans, Winston steps out of the bathroom with another glass. Amelia stands a little apart.)*

AMELIA. I have to go look for work today.

JAMIE. One drink. A toast.

AMELIA. I don't think I'll make a really stellar impression if I walk into Elephant & Castle bobbing and weaving like a wino. *(Jamie hands off the glasses to Winston and Amelia. He raises his glass and toasts.)*

JAMIE. All right, my good friends: Here's to our masterpiece. *(They clink glasses. Jamie and Winston drink. Amelia just holds her glass and watches the men. Winston grabs his backpack.)*

WINSTON. I'm out of here.

JAMIE. Tomorrow morning we'll go to Avenue B, we'll pick out a canvas and scrape it.

WINSTON. *(On his way out the door.)* Sad truth, you know, this is probably the most interesting thing I've ever done. *(The door slams, and Winston is gone. Jamie runs to Amelia and throws his arms around her, kissing her deeply on the mouth.)*

JAMIE. I thought he'd never leave.

AMELIA. I don't think I can do this. *(Jamie takes her in his arms and starts to lead her to the bedroom.)*

JAMIE. You're coming back here with me.

AMELIA. *(Making a weak effort to resist.)* I have to go look for work.

JAMIE. *(Kissing her all over.)* Just a little roll in the hay. It'll take fifteen minutes tops.

AMELIA. What a romantic you are.

JAMIE. It's my opinion that we should start making babies right this second.

AMELIA. I can't tell you how much that is not an aphrodisiac for me.

JAMIE. It is my fondest desire to populate the world with a million little people running around with your face.

AMELIA. That is the most disturbing thing I've ever heard. *(He wraps his arms around her, clasping her hands in his.)*

JAMIE. Because you've saved my life. Really you have. If it weren't for you, they'd be dragging the Hudson for my body right about now.

AMELIA. Don't be silly.

JAMIE. And I absolutely refuse to let you get away. Hey, I've got a great idea, why don't you marry me? *(Antically, Jamie gets down on his knees in front of Amelia.)*

AMELIA. Would you get up off your knees right this instant?

JAMIE. Make an honest man out of me.

AMELIA. I think it's been conclusively proven this morning that you are absolutely *not* an honest man.

JAMIE. Come on, Amelia, what do you say, be a sport.

AMELIA. Why don't we wait till we have more than a dime to our collective names?

JAMIE. If everything goes according to plan that should be by the first of May. So June, then? Everybody loves a June wedding.

AMELIA. *(Stares at him closely.)* We're not really going to do this, are we?

JAMIE. You know what's the most amazing thing about this painting? Not the money. It's that your hands-down breathtaking face will be hanging on somebody's wall. And a hundred years from now, people will stare at that canvas, and they'll be able to see exactly how hands-down breathtaking you are to me right at this moment. *(Despite herself, she melts in his gaze. She smiles shyly at him.)*
AMELIA. I guess I don't really have a choice then, do I? *(He wraps his arms very tightly around her, enveloping her utterly in an embrace.)*
JAMIE. I've got you now.
AMELIA. *(Trapped in his embrace.)* Okay, okay, you win. Just give me a minute, all right? *(He relinquishes his grip. He moves toward the bedroom, gazing at her all the way.)*
JAMIE. Look at you. Even when I'm not looking at you I'm looking at you. *(He disappears into the bedroom. She stares after him a moment. She pulls the robe tighter around her. She walks toward the bedroom. The lights fade.)*

Scene 2

It's Saturday night around 11:30. The floor and table lamps cast a spotty glow across the apartment. The easel is leaned up against the wall by the kitchen.

Winston stands at the work table sharpening his pencils with his paring knife. He wears a white T-shirt and the same paint-spattered sweatpants.

Amelia shakes out her hands, hopping up and down on both feet.

AMELIA. I've never done anything like this before.
WINSTON. You're not chickening out on me, are you?
AMELIA. I haven't ruled out the possibility.

WINSTON. Would you feel, um, less weird if Jamie were here?

AMELIA. *(Stares aghast at him.)* I think I can say with complete authority that I'd feel way *more* weird if Jamie were here.

WINSTON. Okay, well, just, you know, asking. *(Winston throws a blanket over the chair.)*

AMELIA. Me sitting here naked and you sketching me and Jamie watching? I don't think I'd ever get over that.

WINSTON. *(Nods, embarrassed.)* Right, point taken.

AMELIA. *(With a grim determination.)* I'm going to go into the bedroom and take off my clothes now.

WINSTON. Okay, whatever you want. *(Amelia strides with purpose through the beads and into the bedroom. Winston darts around the room, switching off all the lights.)*

AMELIA. *(From the bedroom.)* The idea of doing something like this never crosses my mind. Even when I'm stone-cold broke, I see these fliers posted at the laundromat, "Models Wanted for Life Drawing Class," I can't even bring myself to tear off the phone number.

WINSTON. Some people are just, you know, shy. Nothing to be ashamed of. *(Amelia strides out through the beads, red-faced, fully clothed.)*

AMELIA. All right, clearly I'm still completely dressed.

WINSTON. Maybe you'd, um, like to have a drink?

AMELIA. That is the most brilliant idea ever. *(Quickly, Amelia goes to the cabinets and starts looking for alcohol.)*

WINSTON. See, um, every now and then I say the right thing.

AMELIA. Do we have anything besides the vodka?

WINSTON. I bought some Maker's Mark last night.

AMELIA. Fancy. *(Amelia locates the Maker's Mark and hauls it down from the cupboard.)*

WINSTON. Yeah, I had a supper of, um, bourbon and pork-flavored ramen noodles, I'm a real bon vivant.

AMELIA. I assume the glasses are still in the tub. *(Bottle in hand, Amelia heads into the bathroom.)*

WINSTON. You know, this is just a preliminary sketch. You could easily, um, keep your clothes on tonight and then we could work up to, right, the other stuff, you know, later. *(Amelia has appeared in the bathroom doorway. She pours a glass from the bottle and takes a big belt.)*

AMELIA. But if I'm going to do it then I might as well do it, right? *(She slaps the bottle and glass down on the table, kicks off her shoes, quickly unstraps her dress, lets it fall to the floor, and in a businesslike manner yanks off her underwear. Utterly naked in front of him, she gives him a workmanlike gesture of completion.)*

WINSTON. *(Kind of at a loss.)* Okay, well, um, great.

AMELIA. *(Hands on her hips.)* Now what?

WINSTON. *(Very nervously.)* Oh. Just sit. Right here. Then you'll be, um, under the skylight, you know, with the moon coming down.

AMELIA. Pretty picture. *(She plops down in the chair. He pulls the rope that removes the cover from the skylight. The moon pours onto her naked body. She stares up at the light in panic.)*

WINSTON. Credeaux used pretty much all natural light. So, the skylight, and, um, the moon, and we're good to go. *(He goes over to her, posing her, careful but abstracted. She stares nervously up at him. He considers her, frowning a little.)* Are you, um, feeling more comfortable now?

AMELIA. *(With more brio than she feels.)* If I could have the whiskey by my side. *(Winston gets the Maker's Mark from the table and pours her a glass.)*

WINSTON. Actually it might be great to have you holding a whiskey glass in the picture, it'll make you look that much more like a prostitute.

AMELIA. *(Stares at him.)* What a tremendously unhelpful thing to say.

WINSTON. *(Deeply mortified.)* Gotcha. *(He prepares his sketch pad and pencils. He starts to sketch her. She shifts in her seat, deeply aware of her own nakedness. A very awkward moment.)*

AMELIA. *(To fill a space.)* So Winston: Did you always want to be a painter?

WINSTON. *(With a nervous laugh.)* Um. I guess. I was always drawing. Even when I was, you know, little. It helped me get through school, which I always found, I mean, either boring or, um, annoying.

AMELIA. And your parents? Did they encourage your budding genius?

WINSTON. *(With a laugh.)* My dad, you know, delivers refrigerators and buys lottery tickets. My mom sits at home and complains about my dad. But she'd always get me whatever I asked her for, you know, oils and brushes and stuff. So she was real supportive in her way. *(Amelia sips from the glass and watches Winston watching her, making a lame attempt to be a little less self-conscious about her utterly exposed body.)*

WINSTON. But I call her up sometimes, I tell her I'm broke, she says, "Why don't you come back to Pelham, there are plenty of openings at the telephone company." And then I have to pound my head against the wall for a few hours. My dad wanted me to go into the army.

AMELIA. Get out of town.

WINSTON. That was because when I took the SAT's I didn't even bother to open the booklet, I just, you know, made pretty designs in the ovals with my number two pencil. Lucky I got the scholarship to art school, otherwise right now I'd be on some peacekeeping mission in Croatia.

AMELIA. But here you are. You've found your calling.

WINSTON. Yeah, well, I guess that's one way to be sure you've found your calling. When you pretty much royally suck at everything else. *(Looks up at her.)* Your folks happy you're a singer?

AMELIA. *(With a laugh.)* Happy? I guess. When I was six years old, my mother dressed me up in a silver lamé jumpsuit with sparkles all over, and then she drove me to the Danbury Fair, where I sang a medley from *Annie* at the top of my lungs and somersaulted into a bale of hay. I won a fifty-dollar gift certificate redeemable at any Kay-Bee Toy Store.

WINSTON. Do you have, you know, any pictures of that?

AMELIA. You will never, ever see them. But the only reason my mom went to all that trouble is I wanted it so badly. Both my parents, they've always bent over backwards for me. Even now, they don't even really like the kind of stuff I sing, but a couple times a year they'll pile into the Camry and drive into the city and pay for parking and squeeze into the Lakeside Lounge next to all the NYU kids trying to score, and they're just beaming with pride.

WINSTON. You're very, you know, lucky. *(He turns over a page in his pad. She looks up at him and leans in, suddenly focused on him and much less conscious of her nakedness.)*

AMELIA. *(With a surge of intensity.)* When I first came to New York, I'd cold-call club managers and record executives every day, I'd stick fliers up on street lamps and phone booths from Battery Park all the way up to Columbus Circle, I'd stop total strangers on the street and demand that they come to our gigs. I was an asshole, but I sure had *energy.*

WINSTON. *(Smiles at her.)* Yeah, I know that drill.

AMELIA. *(Very thoughtfully.)* But now I'm so desperate to earn a living at my singing that little by little I'm sapping all the joy out of it. I feel like I'm running a marathon against my own disillusion and exhaustion, and lately I have the creeping suspicion that I'm going to lose. And in my rare moments of honesty I have to admit that if anything was going to happen for me it probably would've happened by now.

WINSTON. But what would you do instead?

AMELIA. *(Thinks, then, fondly.)* I had this great chorus teacher at Ridgefield Elementary School. Miss Volino. She died a couple years ago. My mom sent me the obituary. Turns out she wanted to be an opera singer when she was young, moved to New York right out of high school, pounded the pavement for a few years but nothing ever came of it.

WINSTON. Some people are just, you know, unlucky. *(Amelia leans forward in her chair. She's totally wrapped up in Winston and the conversation and has lost any trace of self-consciousness.)*

AMELIA. When you're a kid you don't look at adults that way, it never occurs to you that they've been ... thwarted. But maybe that wasn't it, maybe one day she just realized what she wanted most in the world was to teach a bunch of fifth-graders to sing "This Land is Your Land." Maybe she had absolutely no regrets.

WINSTON. *(Lightly antic.)* But you don't have to worry about any of that. Jamie's going to make you a star.

AMELIA. *(Suddenly very incisive.)* Listen: Do you ever feel that there's something maybe a little suspicious in the way Jamie thinks we're both so brilliant? Given how little either one of us has actually managed to accomplish thus far?

WINSTON. I'm not quite, um, I'm not sure what you mean.

AMELIA. It's just, the reasons Jamie so fervently insists that we're geniuses, sometimes I think they have a whole lot more to do with him than they have to do with us. You know?

WINSTON. *(Nods, looks down.)* The thought has, I guess, crossed my mind.

AMELIA. *(Takes a swig of Maker's Mark.)* And I can't bear the thought of myself years from now still counting my tips so every few weeks I can belt out a couple tunes in some grimy club on Ludlow. And I can't bear the thought of myself years from now miles away from here only singing in the shower. No matter what I do, I'm terrified I'm already turning into a shadow of myself, and I can't bear to watch the life drain out of me, I don't want to be wrecked by what I've become.

WINSTON. *(Suddenly very passionate.)* But it's not about being a genius, is it? I mean, if you know you have a calling ... well, then, the whole point is to be tremendously vigilant, be ruthless in exposing your weaknesses, flagellate yourself until you overcome them. And even if after all that, the world doesn't want you — so what? At least you did what you were called to do.

AMELIA. *(Astonished.)* Listen to you.

WINSTON. But if you deny the things that you love, if you turn your back on them — well, then, maybe you can still be content, but there's no getting around the fact that your life will be in some way essentially broken and hollow and just plain wrong. *(He stares at her very intensely. She shifts nervously in her chair.)*

AMELIA. All of a sudden I feel really naked.

WINSTON. Oh, here, um, maybe this'll help. *(Affectlessly Winston sets his pad and pencil on the floor, gets up, pulls off his T-shirt, and steps out of his sweatpants and boxers. He stands in front of her, naked except for his tube socks. Then he sits back down, puts his pad back on his lap, and resumes sketching. She stares flabbergasted at him.)*

AMELIA. Did you actually think that was going to make me less tense?

WINSTON. *(Looks up at her, surprised.)* Oh, well, I just thought, um, turnabout is fair play, if I can dish it out I'd better be able to take it, right?

AMELIA. I truly hope that someday you'll be able to return to your home planet.

WINSTON. *(Utterly mortified again.)* Gosh, I just, actually, you know, I kind of *like* being naked while I'm drawing, when I'm alone here that's what I usually, oh hell, you don't want to know that, I'll just put my — *(He reaches for his boxers.)*

AMELIA. *(Decides to roll with it.)* Don't bother, really, it's fine.

WINSTON. No, I'm freaking you out, I can tell.

AMELIA. Whatever makes you comfortable.

WINSTON. Oh. All right. Whatever you say. *(He nods and happily goes back to sketching. She rolls her eyes and takes a big swig of Maker's Mark. Winston considers her closely.)* Actually if you could lean forward like you were. *(Amelia leans forward in her chair. Winston nods.)* Like that. *(Amelia can't help but laugh at the ridiculousness of the situation. Winston allows himself to laugh a little too. Then he goes back to sketching. She thinks a moment.)*

AMELIA. Jamie asked me to marry him again today.

WINSTON. Hasn't he, um, been asking you that every day?

AMELIA. But today was the first day I seriously considered the question.

WINSTON. *(Looks up at her, surprised.)* Oh, gosh, I guess, congratulations are in order then, maybe?

AMELIA. He doesn't know I'm seriously considering it. In fact you and I are the only two people in the world who know I'm seriously considering it.

WINSTON. *(Getting a little nervous.)* Oh. Boy. Well. Should you really be — ? I'm not sure you should be telling me this, my roommate and all, plus I hate having any kind of secrets, my stomach gets all tied in knots —

AMELIA. *(Cuts him off, very intently.)* Can I ask you some questions about Jamie?

WINSTON. *(With a flustered laugh.)* Hmm, boy, that's an even worse idea, isn't it? Because you're really putting me right in the middle of — not to mention the fact that he could walk in here, you know, any —

AMELIA. *(Stares pointedly at him.)* He's covering Janelle's shift at the bar, he won't be home till four. And if he *does* suddenly barge in, I guarantee he'll be way more concerned about why you're sitting here in your birthday suit than by anything we might be *saying* to each other.

WINSTON. Okay, point taken.

AMELIA. *(Leans in to him a little.)* So can I ask you a few questions about him?

WINSTON. *(Clears his throat anxiously.)* Well, I mean, you can *ask*. But I'll choose whether or not to answer on, um, a question-by-question basis.

AMELIA. Fair enough.

WINSTON. Okay.

AMELIA. Did Jamie have a lot of girlfriends before me?

WINSTON. See, um, already we're on shaky ground here.

AMELIA. It's a perfectly harmless question.

WINSTON. *(Squirming in his chair.)* In so many ways you'd be better off asking Jamie about this.

AMELIA. *(Evenly but firmly.)* Jamie also refuses to answer this question. He simply says that the moment he laid eyes on me he was new-baptized. Which is sweet but also really elusive. So I'm forced to consult other sources. *(She stares at him. He attempts to meet her gaze, for the first time feeling pretty naked himself.)*

WINSTON. *(Choosing his words carefully.)* This girl Susan, she was a photographer. And then he was with Joyce for about a year, she was, um, she was a poet, she was kind of depressing. And then there was this other girl, I forget her name, she had really crinkly hair. So a few. Several. Sure.

AMELIA. And did he think they were all utter, total geniuses, just like he thinks I am?

WINSTON. Oh, God.

AMELIA. Well?

WINSTON. I can't answer that one.

AMELIA. Actually I think you already have.

WINSTON. *(Runs his fingers through his hair.)* See, that's the problem with this game, you kind of hold all the cards. I think we really ought to, you know, stop now.

AMELIA. Just one more question: Do you think Jamie is in love with me?

WINSTON. *(Suddenly very exasperated.)* What the hell am I supposed to know about that?

AMELIA. I'm sure you've got an opinion, so I'm interested.

WINSTON. Whatever I think doesn't matter one bit.

AMELIA. So it doesn't matter one bit if you tell me.

WINSTON. You're trying, um, to trick me here.

30

AMELIA. I already have. See, this is another one of those questions where not answering is also an answer. *(Her eyes are locked on him. Finally he nods, looking right up at her, meeting her gaze.)*

WINSTON. No. I don't think he's in love with you. I think he's just looking at you, because you're so pretty. *(Amelia lets the truth of this wash over her. She nods thoughtfully.)*

AMELIA. Well. Thank you. You've been extremely helpful.

WINSTON. *(Deeply upset.)* Then why do I feel like I've committed a crime?

AMELIA. *(A little arch.)* Hey, at least he thinks I'm pretty, right?

WINSTON. Give me a break. Of course he thinks you're pretty. You already know that about yourself.

AMELIA. *(An attempt at levity.)* Well, I think you're awfully pretty too. You're one of those boys, you've got a secret kind of beauty. Which is the most dangerous kind of beauty really.

WINSTON. *(Deeply uncomfortable.)* I'm not, um, I'm not really sure what you mean.

AMELIA. *(Utterly forthright.)* It's just, when your beauty makes itself apparent to a girl, if she doesn't watch out she can be fooled into thinking that she discovered it.

WINSTON. Oh. Well. Hmm. Thank you. *(He stares down at his crumpled clothes on the floor, longing to cover himself up again.)*

AMELIA. Jamie thinks you might be gay.

WINSTON. *(Laughs lamely.)* Yeah, I sort of figured Jamie might think that.

AMELIA. *(A little waspishly.)* Well, who do you like better, girls or boys?

WINSTON. *(With a weak smile.)* That, you know, that's like asking a man crawling across the Sahara desert whether he prefers Poland Spring or Deer Park.

AMELIA. *(Completely fascinated.)* Really.

WINSTON. *(Turns to her, suddenly intense.)* You don't have to — I'm fine, really — I grew up watching my brothers maul cheerleaders in the back seat of our Malibu Classic, or I look at you and Jamie wrapped around each other on his futon, theoretically I understand what you all get out of it but I've never been able to see how it applies to me.

AMELIA. Poor guy.

31

WINSTON. *(Fixes her with a withering look.)* Hey, it's not like I'm some kind of, you know, *neophyte*, I've had my share of — any time I feel like having sex, you know, I just go out and do it.

AMELIA. You don't have to explain anything to me.

WINSTON. *(On a tear now.)* And it's fun, you know, you go to a bar and talk to people, you get to ask them all about their lives, find out what it's like to grow up in Joliet or St. Louis, plus you get to see any number of interesting apartments all over New York City. Once I even went to Queens, I'd never been there before.

AMELIA. Good for you.

WINSTON. But do you know what my favorite part of the whole thing always is? Riding back in the cab, the city all spotlit and flickering, some power ballad playing on the radio, I'm heading home safe and sound, I had a little adventure, and I got away scot-free.

AMELIA. *(Shakes her head.)* One of these days some poor fool is gonna fall head over heels in love with you, and then you won't know which end is up.

WINSTON. *(Tremendously annoyed now.)* Oh, please. There's this girl at the library, we work a bunch of shifts together. And it can get deadly in there, so to pass the time we start telling *stories*, right? About our *lives*. And for some reason people have this tendency to think that when I talk to them it *means* something. That I'm saying something *important. (She leans in even closer to him now, amazed by his vehemence.)* When actually I think words are nothing more than chatter, you use them to plug *holes*, you toss them out like pennies as you're walking down the street, you don't even turn around to see if anybody bothered to pick them up.

AMELIA. Wow.

WINSTON. *(With a deep sense of disgust.)* And so this *girl*, right, she thinks because we *talked*, because we told each other *stories*, now I *owe* her something. And I can feel her across the table from me eight hours a day, yearning, pining, it's getting so annoying that I can't even *look* at her. *(With a flat finality.)* Some people are just supposed to be alone. *(She bursts into laughter. He stares at her, a bit put out.)* What are you laughing at?

AMELIA. You.

WINSTON. I'm not sure what I — I wasn't trying to be funny, I don't think.

AMELIA. I know. You just are. Because it's so transparent, the way you talk, you're the most heartsick creature in the entire universe.

WINSTON. Really I don't know what, um, gives you that impression.

AMELIA. Admit it. What you want most in the world is for someone to sit down in front of you and look at you in such a way that you abandon yourself completely, you throw over everything you've been up till this point in your life. And you look back at them, and reflected in their eyes you see the entire rest of your life set out in front of you.

WINSTON. *(A moment, then, looks up at her.)* That, you know, that would be wonderful. *(Amelia and Winston stare at each other for an extremely charged and dangerous moment.)*

AMELIA. I'm pregnant.

WINSTON. I don't, I, uh — what?

AMELIA. I'm barely a month gone. Jamie doesn't know yet.

WINSTON. *(His head in his hands.)* Why do you keep *telling* me all this stuff?

AMELIA. That's why I seriously considered his marriage proposal this morning.

WINSTON. *(Utterly exasperated now.)* I should go pound my head against the wall to see if I can somehow dislodge all this new information from my brain. That was a real genius move. Haven't you guys ever heard of birth control?

AMELIA. *(Very intensely.)* Yeah, but Jamie gets so enthusiastic that a lot of the time precautions do not get taken. In hindsight I'm beginning to suspect that Jamie's so enthusiastic at least partly *because* he doesn't want me to take precautions. Because then I might accidentally get pregnant. And then I might seriously consider his marriage proposal. *(She polishes off the Maker's Mark in her glass and pours some more.)*

WINSTON. Isn't it, you know, a little dangerous for you to be drinking so much right now?

AMELIA. *(Looks up at him.)* It would be horribly dangerous if I wasn't already pretty sure I was gonna do what I'm now absolutely sure I'm gonna do.

WINSTON. *(Stares closely at her.)* Because of what I said?

AMELIA. *(A moment, then:)* Maybe a little.

33

WINSTON. What are you doing to me?

AMELIA. *(With a surge of emotion.)* Well, what am I supposed to — if you've got any bright ideas, please, help me out here. Could you? Because I can't — I — *(Winston stares intently at her. His pad sits forgotten in his lap.)*

WINSTON. *(Very intensely.)* Hey, hey, don't. Please, don't, because I — look — I walk around this city, every day I see people desperately clinging to each other, they couldn't figure out in fifty years what you figured out in six months. *(His hands are wrapped around each other. She sits very straight in her chair and watches him, her eyes welling up, her body trembling.)* And you're decent enough to be twisted into knots about this but you're also, um, courageous enough to know that in the end it's the only thing to do. It'll spare the kid and it'll save you and, you know, maybe it'll even save Jamie if he lets it. *(She puts her hand to her mouth, her face flushed, her eyes watery.)* But don't you dare start thinking that all the life's draining out of you, that years from now you're gonna be wrecked by what you became. Because, you know, when I look at you I see a girl who's keen and hungry and so, I mean, vital that frankly it kind of scares me. That's, um, what I see. And I'm, you know, I'm looking really closely. *(Tentatively she rises and steps toward him, terrified and hopeful. He laughs nervously. The corners of his mouth turn up slightly.)*

AMELIA. What is that? A smile? *(She looks down at him, almost sick with longing. He stares up at her. Slowly she walks toward him. She leans down to him and puts one hand on the back of his head. He reaches up toward her, lays his hands gently on her cheeks and kisses her mouth. Their bodies move in and out of the moonlight.)*

End of Act One

ACT TWO

Scene 1

Three P.M. on a Thursday in April. A lame and half-hearted attempt has been made to tidy up the apartment but even clean the place looks messy.

Jamie shifts nervously on the balls of his feet. He wears the same dress pants but a different shirt.

Winston stands a few feet away from him tapping his fingers against the kitchen counter. He has dressed up for the occasion, which means faded black jeans instead of sweats and a frayed dress shirt.

Both Winston and Jamie are sitting on a mountain of tension.

Tess stands between them. It's impossible to pin down her exact age. She is dressed very smartly but not ostentatiously. She is flighty and emotional and regal. Her hand is at her heart.

TESS. I'm a little out of breath.
JAMIE. You were enormously courageous to attempt a fifth-floor walk-up.
TESS. I did not make a practical choice of shoes this morning.
JAMIE. This is why I thought it would be much more expedient to bring the painting up to your townhouse.
TESS. *(Shakes her head, with a laugh.)* Ever since my heart attack they've kept me locked up in that house. All day long it's just me and the dog and Inez. Every now and then the phone rings, it's someone who wants me to change my long-distance carrier, I'm so

desperate to relieve the monotony, I stay on the line with them for hours going over payment plans.

JAMIE. You protest too much.

TESS. And I just feel like I'm rattling around that place now that Gil's died. I beg the kids to come over, but as soon as they show up I can't wait for them to leave. Russ only cares about football, and it's anyone's guess what Tracy cares about. I take them to the study, I say, look at this Rousseau I just bought, they curl up in front of the TV and go to sleep.

JAMIE. You're out practically every night. I can't flip through a newspaper without seeing your name in bold letters.

TESS. *(Waves it away with her hand.)* Benefits. What a thrill. You sit at a table with a bunch of hateful people, you take two bites out of a rubbery chicken breast, some second-tier Atlantic City crooner sings one song, and then you write a check big enough to buy housing for the entire population of Biloxi, Mississippi.

WINSTON. Boy.

TESS. And you *know* ninety-five percent of the money you give them will just be used to defray the cost of *having* the benefit in the first place. And then you're riding home with your gift bag full of little shampoos and facial cleansers, and you can't help but feel like you've been had.

WINSTON. Still, you know, a free meal sounds nice.

TESS. Aren't you sweet. One reason I was so excited to visit you — years ago, whenever friends would come to town, I'd always bring them to the Village. You'd sit in a coffee house and watch these unbelievable people stroll past. That was the key to this neighborhood, all the coffee, it made everyone so wonderfully ... agitated.

WINSTON. Would you like, um, a glass of water?

TESS. Yes, that would be lovely, wouldn't it? *(Winston ducks into the bathroom.)*

JAMIE. Are you completely recovered from the stairs?

TESS. *(Waves it away with her hand.)* Just a poor choice of shoes, I should've worn my flats. Now, Jamie, you know I don't waffle and I don't haggle. If I like what I see, I'll make you a non-negotiable offer. And I'll leave you with a check, and I'll leave here with a painting. *(Winston comes back out with a water glass, which he hands to Tess.)*

36

JAMIE. I'm completely familiar with your mode of operation. Remember, I used to watch you with my father.

TESS. And it's absolutely kismet that you have a Credeaux. Believe it or not, I already own one of his paintings.

WINSTON. *(Immediately interested.)* Jamie mentioned something about that.

TESS. *(Switching into oratorical mode.)* When I was eighteen years old, my aunt Charlotte took me to Paris. We were staying with her friend Marianne. And over the bureau in her guest bedroom was this still life. Just a comb and a bottle of wine. Yet in the painting they seemed like the most exquisite objects in the world.

WINSTON. It's the economy of his brushwork and the quality of the light.

TESS. That's right. And then I saw the signature: Jean-Paul Credeaux. Marianne told me that her favorite uncle was a cardsharp, and the painting had been given to him by one of his marks to cover a gambling debt. She wanted to make me a present of it, but I insisted on paying. It was one of the first paintings I ever bought.

WINSTON. *(Getting very excited.)* That's how almost all his paintings were circulated — to pay back money he lost at cards. He only sold five or six canvases outright in his entire life. And there was one commissioned portrait of some provincial corporal's wife.

TESS. *(Fixes him in her gaze.)* My goodness, you know an awful lot about Jean-Paul Credeaux.

JAMIE. Winston knows an awful lot about practically every painter. He's an encyclopedia.

TESS. But still. Credeaux is tremendously obscure. Even your father had barely heard of him. Or at least that's what he pretended. Because now it appears that he had a Credeaux of his own.

JAMIE. You know how secretive my father was, he didn't even tell his closest friends about all the paintings he had.

TESS. Oh, yes. And now all of a sudden they're finding all these canvases — nobody even knew they *existed*. I may queer my deal here, Jamie, but if you hold on to your Credeaux for a few more years, heaven knows what you'll get for it.

JAMIE. *(With tremendous gravity.)* The thing about my father, he was a truly generous man, he just didn't want anyone to know it.

And I think he bought the painting for you, but he gave it to me, in the hopes that we might be able to help each other, that we might be able to continue his work now that he's gone.

TESS. What a lovely boy you are.

JAMIE. *(Beaming.)* I'll get everything ready. That'll give Winston a chance to tell you all about his own brilliant work. He's a genius artist himself. You're gonna be paying top dollar for one of his paintings someday. *(Jamie sets up the chair and the easel. Tess eyes Winston.)*

TESS. So you're a painter.

WINSTON. One more semester and, um, I'm done with my master's.

TESS. I went to drawing school when I was your age. I was a miserable failure: Everyone I drew came out looking like they had either gigantism or rickets. If I have any talent at all, it's only for art appreciation.

JAMIE. That's an extremely important thing.

TESS. It's such small potatoes next to what a real artist does. You create something from nothing. All I do is walk around, and look at things and decide whether or not they're beautiful. That's awfully frivolous, don't you think?

WINSTON. Oh, gosh, I mean, no, not at all. Because, I guess, that's the same thing painters do, right, we walk around, something catches our attention, and we want to, you know, *preserve* it.

TESS. *(Deeply touched.)* One of the very last drawings I did was of my husband. It was my wedding gift to him. He kept it in his office, and when he died I had it reframed, and I hung it over the living room mantel. Not because it's a good drawing: If you were kind you'd call it amateurish, and if you were honest you'd say it was embarrassing. *(Her hands are shaking slightly. Jamie and Winston stare at her.)* But I can read in every line how much I adored him then, how overwhelming he was to me. And it's sad, of course, because now he's gone, but it's also quite wonderful to be able to see precisely what I saw in him, to look at what was there.

WINSTON. That sounds, you know, like a really nice gift.

TESS. *(Considers him very closely.)* So: Do you have any paintings of your own here that I can look at?

JAMIE. *(Gestures to the work table.)* He has a whole stack of them right over there.

WINSTON. *(Flushing red.)* Oh, um, you don't have to.

TESS. I'm truly interested. You may think I'm a stick-in-the-mud, but I have nearly as many living painters in my collection as dead ones.

WINSTON. *(With an awkward laugh.)* That, you know, that's kind of inspiring to hear.

JAMIE. I'll go get the canvas. *(Jamie disappears through the beads. Winston goes to the work table and pulls off the burlap that covers his canvases. He flips through them, considering nervously.)*

TESS. And I'm always ravenous for a new discovery. I bought an Eric Fischl when he was in his cradle for pennies. I'm still the envy of the neighborhood for that one. Maybe I can walk out of here today with one old master and one bright young thing. *(He picks out a painting and holds it out toward Tess.)*

WINSTON. This is, um, for my thesis. *(She takes the canvas from him and holds it out at arm's length from her face, examining it carefully. He steps away from her and taps his fingers on the table anxiously.)*

TESS. *(As lightly as possible.)* Well, this is rather a bit of a mess, now, isn't it?

WINSTON. *(Stares at her.)* I'm sorry?

TESS. This whole collage effect: Obviously you're hugely influenced by David Salle.

WINSTON. Well, um, I wouldn't go so far as to say *influenced*.

TESS. And these panels, are they supposed to be pastiche of Vlaminck?

WINSTON. *(Clearing his throat.)* I've been kind of obsessed with the Fauvists, so, um.

TESS. *(Riding right over him.)* It seems that you want to be a classical naturalist but you're too self-conscious, so you've tried to be a post-modernist but your heart's not in it, so what you've wound up with is an uncomfortable melding of the two. Don't you think? *(She stares at him rather brightly. His hands twist around each other.)*

WINSTON. Oh. Huh. Well. *(She becomes aware that she has gone too far and tries to backpedal.)*

TESS. Which is not to say it's untalented. The brushwork is excellent even if it is a little overdetermined, and you certainly don't suffer from a lack of ideas. If I were to look you up in five or ten years, I wouldn't be at all surprised to discover that you'd actually developed into someone. (*A pause.*) I hope I haven't hurt your feelings.

WINSTON. Oh, no, um, don't be silly, I have very, you know, thick skin. (*He takes the painting from her and stuffs it back under the burlap.*)

TESS. (*A relieved smile.*) Good for you. And I know how you artists are, I'm sure you're much tougher on your own work than I could ever be.

WINSTON. (*Moving toward the hanging beads.*) You bet ... hey, uh, Jamie, you need any help back there?

JAMIE. (*From the bedroom.*) Here I come! (*Tess turns away, covering her eyes.*)

TESS. Oh, no, I'm too nervous! I can't look, I absolutely can't look! (*Jamie passes through the beads with the canvas and sets it down on the easel.*)

JAMIE. Feast your eyes on this. (*Tess turns and looks at the canvas. Winston and Jamie stare straight out, unable to look at the painting or at each other. For an agonizing moment Tess stares at the painting, her face completely unreadable.*)

TESS. It's marvelous, isn't it? (*Tess puts her hand to her mouth and her eyes water. Winston and Jamie both exhale almost audibly.*)

JAMIE. We sure think so. (*Tess moves closer to the painting. Her instinct is to touch it but she suppresses it as best she can: It doesn't belong to her yet.*)

TESS. He's even more brilliant with the moon than he is with the sun! Look at how it begins right up here as a sharp ray of light and then it ever so gently diffuses through the room!

WINSTON. (*With suppressed pride.*) Yeah, you know, I love that, too.

TESS. And see the way it reflects off the glass in her hand! It's a perfect little prism!

JAMIE. (*Shrugs his shoulders.*) I don't know a damn thing about painting and even *I* love it.

TESS. And the economy of that glass! A tiny dash of fuchsia and this entire corporeal object is utterly evoked! There isn't a wasted brushstroke anywhere, is there?

WINSTON. I know, it almost feels like, you know, he's afraid he's about to run out of paint.

TESS. (*Hand to her heart.*) And the girl! Look at the girl! You

40

know, I've never seen him work with the human form before! Only those reproductions in the magazine, and they don't do him a bit of justice! The limbs, how unbelievably supple, and the way her feet curl around the chair — ! *(Winston and Jamie are careful enough not to look at each other but are nonetheless sharing a moment of complicitous triumph as Tess has her paroxysms of joy.)*

JAMIE. She truly is unbelievably extraordinary. *(Tess suddenly turns to Jamie, takes him by the hand, and leads him over to the painting.)*

TESS. It's not her. Don't you see, Jamie, it's not her at all! You could pass by that girl on the street every day and not even notice her! It's all about the way he *looks* at her! The courage he sees in her! And the despair! The way that she's got her chin raised up so proudly but there's something lost behind her eyes!

JAMIE. *(A little taken aback.)* What I forgot about you, Tess, when you look at a painting, you really *look* at a painting, don't you? *(Tess releases her hold on Jamie and stands about an inch away from the painting, poring over every detail. Winston and Jamie watch intently.)*

TESS. You know what's really stunning, it's this right here, where the moonlight hits her hair, it's almost unbearably vibrant!

JAMIE. Yeah, wow, how about that?

TESS. *(Peering very closely at it.)* Oooh — there's something awfully familiar about this.

WINSTON. I think he used that trope in, you know, some of his still lifes.

TESS. No, it's not from a Credeaux. It's from someone else's painting.

WINSTON. Well, he was largely influenced by Matisse.

TESS. *(With a laugh.)* Isn't it funny, I want to say it's like Abstract Expressionism.

JAMIE. *(Very jovially.)* Well, who knows, right?

TESS. *(Her eyes narrowing.)* No, you know what? I think it *is* Abstract Expressionism.

WINSTON. *(Laughs very nervously.)* That, you know, that's kind of a stretch.

TESS. *(With a new gravity.)* In fact, it's Helen Frankenthaler. It's a direct quote from *Mountains and Sea*.

JAMIE. *(Shifts uneasily on his feet.)* I don't think I know that painting.

41

TESS. For shame, Jamie. It's one of the great paintings of — Winston, you must know what I'm talking about. Do you see this orange line here, next to this blue tinge that's set against this green wash? It's *Mountains and Sea*. It's precisely the same vocabulary! It's almost exactly the same brushstrokes! *(Winston's face goes very white. Hanging back a bit, Jamie isn't quite sure what's going on but senses that it isn't good.)*
WINSTON. I'm not sure that I, um, see it quite as, uh, strongly as you do.
TESS. What on earth is Abstract Expressionism doing in a Credeaux portrait?
JAMIE. So, what, are you saying that he was influenced by —
TESS. *(Very impatiently.)* Of course not, he *couldn't* have been influenced by *Mountains and Sea*, Helen Frankenthaler didn't paint it until 1952, and Credeaux was long dead by then.
JAMIE. *(A moment, then:)* Aha.
TESS. I hate to say it, Jamie, but this could very well be a forgery.
JAMIE. Tess, you know how thoroughly my father vetted everything that passed through his hands. I can't imagine he'd let anything slip by. Particularly on a painting that he bought for himself.
TESS. Anyone can make a mistake. Do you have all the paperwork on this?
JAMIE. Of course I do, I mean, not *on* me, everything's in my dad's files —
TESS. Why don't you messenger it up to me? I'll have some people go over it in detail.
JAMIE. — if it's still even *in* the files, Gail has been systematically *shredding* all his papers, God knows if they still *exist* —
TESS. I mean, this is for your *own* protection, because if this is a fake then you could sue for a lot of money, you could even maybe throw whoever sold it to your father in *jail* —
WINSTON. *(Suddenly looks up.)* But this doesn't, you know, it doesn't make any sense.
TESS. What doesn't make any sense?
WINSTON. *(Turns to Jamie, very intently.)* I mean, this painting was in your dad's collection for how many years?
JAMIE. *(Slowly and thoughtfully.)* Oh, I don't know. It would have to be five or six years at least.

WINSTON. And practically nobody had even *heard* of Jean-Paul Credeaux till last month. And all these years nobody cared about him. You could buy any one of his paintings for a song, right? So why on earth would anybody bother to forge one?

TESS. *(Stares at Winston.)* You do have a point there.

JAMIE. *(Heads toward the phone.)* I can call Cynthia at my father's office right now.

TESS. *(Turns back to the painting.)* I mean, it could be a plagiarism rather than a forgery. Someone saw one of the Credeaux nudes lying around somewhere and decided to copy it. But that seems awfully unlikely, doesn't it?

WINSTON. Right. If it were a plagiarism, then the technique wouldn't be so studious, would it? I mean, then the whole point would be to make it look as *little* like Credeaux as possible.

TESS. It's his use of light. Don't you think? Nobody could fake that. *(Tess turns back to consider the painting. She desperately wants to believe that it's the real thing.)*

WINSTON. Plus, do you know, there are plenty of these weird synergistic cases where two artists working on different continents, in different decades even, come up with the exact same technique, you know, entirely independently of each other. *(Tess stares at Winston, slowly taking in what he has said. Then she turns and stares at the canvas. She extends her arms toward it.)*

TESS. *(Beside herself with joy.)* He anticipated Abstract Expressionism!

JAMIE. How about that.

TESS. *(Nearly whirling around the room.)* He was a genius! I've always known that! Since I was eighteen years old! And I'm a genius for knowing that he was a genius!

JAMIE. Can't argue with that.

TESS. *(Takes Jamie's hand.)* Oh, Jamie, you have to forgive me. It's just, occasionally in the past I've been taken in by a fraud or two. I get so emotional when I look at paintings, I'm highly susceptible to that sort of thing.

JAMIE. *(Claps her lightly on the arm.)* You were just looking out for me — protecting my investment.

TESS. You're very kind, but it's an insult to your father. It's an insult to you.

JAMIE. No harm, no foul. *(Tess goes to Jamie and embraces him. Then she goes to Winston and embraces him as well.)*

WINSTON. *(A little startled.)* Oh. Hi. *(Tess turns back to the canvas and puts her hand to her heart.)*

TESS. It really is a masterwork, isn't it? The way he gets her to engage our eyes without her even knowing that she's doing it. And the way her arm rests so tenderly right here, right here in this precise spot, it's almost as though she's ... what is she doing? It's like she's ... I can't quite tell what she's ... *(She muses for a long moment. Then she steps back. She lets out a scream. Winston and Jamie both jump nearly a foot in the air.)*

TESS. Oh! Oh! My favorite professor at Smith! He always said: What separates a merely great painting from a true masterpiece — it's that every masterpiece contains a secret between the painter and his subject! And the spectator can only discern this secret through heedful and vigilant meditation and study! And I have discovered the secret of this painting!

WINSTON. Wow, um, that was fast.

TESS. She's pregnant. *(Winston and Jamie stare at Tess for a moment. Then they both turn and look at the painting.)*

JAMIE. Where do — I mean, how do you see that?

TESS. Look at this little line here! Right here, by her abdomen!

WINSTON. That could be, um, any number of things.

TESS. *(Very passionately.)* I don't think so. Because look at the way her arm is resting so tenderly and protectively against her belly.

JAMIE. *(His eyes wide.)* Now I see it.

TESS. And look at how her hand is clenched into a fist, so tightly that there are beads of perspiration falling down the inside of her thigh.

JAMIE. And that's why her chin looks like it's trembling a little.

WINSTON. Oh, gosh, um, hmm.

JAMIE. *(Flush with emotion.)* And that's why there's all that fear in her eyes. She doesn't know what to do. She needs someone to take care of her.

TESS. *(Getting very carried away.)* And look at the fiery strokes of red in her cheeks and the gently throbbing vein in her hand. He presents her with such empathy and such love. It truly is love, isn't it? The way he's looking at her, it's absolutely without question

44

that he's in love with her.

WINSTON. Wow, um, this is really a pretty remarkable painting, isn't it? *(They all stare at the painting in silence for a long moment.)*

TESS. You've given me something tremendous here, you know that. I certainly don't believe in coincidences or fate or, God forbid, God. But I do believe in wheels within wheels. When you're a girl you drop a penny in a stream, and when you're an old woman you see it wash up to shore. And you can look at a painting and suddenly an ordinary day becomes tremendously ... significant. *(Tess is holding her purse very tightly, and her eyes are watering over with tears.)* Because there are so many beautiful things in this world, and I have to tell you, boys, the best possible way to spend your life is to look very closely at as many of them as you can. Just to give them the notice they deserve. And I — *(All of a sudden the front door flies open, and Amelia barrels into the apartment. Her hair is damp, her face is pale, and there are dark pools beneath her eyes.)*

AMELIA. I'm sorry. I couldn't help myself. *(They turn to see her. Her face is twisted into a grimace. Winston and Jamie go over to her, partly out of concern and partly to shield Tess from the sight of her.)*

JAMIE. Hey, hey, sweetie, what are you — you shouldn't be —

AMELIA. *(With a burst of laughter.)* I can't let this happen.

WINSTON. Do you want to, um, lie down, in the back, maybe for a while, because we — *(Tess rises and heads toward them. Jamie goes to her and starts to pull her away from Amelia.)*

TESS. Is everything all right? I feel like I've landed in the middle of —

AMELIA. *(Very intensely.)* I had to come see you, I had to come and *see* this, I had to come *stop* it — *(Amelia moves around Winston and heads right for Tess. Jamie takes Tess more forcefully by the arm.)*

JAMIE. Everything is fine, it's just my girlfriend, things have been crazy around here lately — *(Willfully and defiantly, Amelia pulls Tess back to her and takes her by the hand. Jamie and Winston stare in muted horror.)*

AMELIA. I'm Amelia, I'm Jamie's, I'm Amelia. *(Tess takes Amelia's outstretched hand. Amelia's gaze falls on the painting. Tess follows Amelia's eyes and stares at the canvas. Instinctively she reels back as though she's been slapped. She turns back to consider Amelia's face. Her hands start to shake.)*

TESS. You look like you're about to be sick.

AMELIA. *(Nods, gagging a little.)* There's a very good chance of that. If you'll excuse me. *(Amelia runs into the bathroom and slams the door shut behind her. Winston takes a step backward. Jamie stuffs his hands in his pockets. They both stare out. Tess stands clutching her purse, twisting the straps in her hands.)*

TESS. *(A lost smile.)* I believe the viewing is over for today.

JAMIE. I take full responsibility for this.

TESS. As well you should.

JAMIE. I don't have any money.

TESS. I'm sorry to hear it.

JAMIE. My father didn't leave me anything. *(Tess considers Jamie as though for the first time. She nods.)*

TESS. I can see why. *(Jamie's whole body crumples. Tess allows her gaze to fall on Winston.)*

WINSTON. I, uh, I, um. *(Tess pulls her checkbook and pen from her purse. She gestures to the canvases on the work table.)*

TESS. Winston, I think I do want to buy that little painting you showed me after all.

WINSTON. You don't, I mean, please don't.

TESS. Honestly I'd like to. I'm afraid I underestimated you. You're far more versatile than it appears on first glance. *(Tess stands over the work table and writes a check.)*

WINSTON. You're, you know, you're much too kind.

TESS. You're an excellent investment. I mean it.

WINSTON. I'll need, um, to keep it till June, you know, for my portfolio. *(Tess rips off the check, folds it in half, and hands it to Winston.)*

TESS. No rush. Just send it along once you're through with it. I don't need a receipt. Jamie has my address. *(Tess starts out the door.)*

JAMIE. I wish there was something I could do.

TESS. So do I. *(The door slams and she is gone.)*

JAMIE. I need to talk to Amelia — can you —

WINSTON. *(Nods vigorously.)* I, uh, feel like sitting on the fire escape for a while anyway.

JAMIE. Just for a few minutes.

WINSTON. My head is spinning. *(Winston shoves aside the hanging beads and heads into the bedroom. Jamie stares at the painting for a moment. Slowly his lips curl into a smile. He runs over and knocks on the bathroom door.)*

JAMIE. Come on out, Amelia, you don't have to hide in there … I absolutely refuse to let you blame yourself for any of this. *(There is no response from the bathroom. He starts knocking harder and more insistently.)* Because I'm the one who was awful here, I'm the one who committed a *crime*, and you were trying to stop it, you were trying to save me, and you have, really you have, and I know *everything*, I saw it as soon as I saw the painting, that's how well I know you —

AMELIA. *(From the bathroom.)* You know everything?

JAMIE. We're going to have a baby, aren't we? *(He smiles hopefully. The bathroom door swings open and Amelia stands beneath the transom.)*

AMELIA. And you think that's everything? *(Jamie goes to Amelia and throws his arms around her. Amelia can do nothing but stare out and suffer his embrace.)*

JAMIE. And I know you're terrified about that, and you have every right to be.

AMELIA. Believe me, the baby is the very last thing that I am —

JAMIE. But I want to marry you. You know I've always wanted to. I know you don't think I'm serious but I am.

AMELIA. I know how serious you are. Do you know how awful it is, how serious you are?

JAMIE. I know you think it's impossible, but it's not. I can go full time at the real-estate office. That's not just commission. That's a real salary.

AMELIA. That job makes you nothing but miserable.

JAMIE. And I'll fight my dad's will. Gail will cave so quickly, by the time the baby arrives we'll be rolling in dough.

AMELIA. You're not making any sense.

JAMIE. And you can take care of the baby during the day, and then I'll come home from work and watch her while you go out and sing.

AMELIA. Are you even listening to yourself?

JAMIE. Or I'll bring the baby out to the club, she'll hear her mommy sing and she won't even cry, she'll just drift off to sleep.

AMELIA. That sounds like a terrible plan.

JAMIE. Because suddenly it's crystal clear to me exactly how I should spend my days. I should spend them taking care of you. I should spend them taking care of you and our baby.

AMELIA. *(Struggles a moment, then:)* Except I don't think you love me.

JAMIE. *(Stares at her.)* Now you're talking like a crazy person.

AMELIA. *(With tremendous effort.)* I think you got excited by me is all. And no one had ever gotten so excited by me because, let's face it, no one gets more excited than you. And all that was so overwhelming so I got overwhelmed. All I think we've been is just excitable and overwhelmed. And the rest of it I think we just made up to make ourselves feel better.

JAMIE. I'm in love with you, that's all.

AMELIA. Anyway, in the end all you want is some girl to wrap her arms around you and protect you from your father who's dead anyway.

JAMIE. I know I'm a mess about my father.

AMELIA. And it infects everything you touch.

JAMIE. Right, screw him, I should leave him in the dust, I should build a family for myself, I should do it right, that would be the best revenge, don't you think?

AMELIA. I just really don't think *revenge* should be the operative — *(Cuts herself off, very intently.)* And I can't shake the idea that this is all some kind of *scheme*. That you *planned* for this to happen.

JAMIE. *(Brought up short.)* How can you possibly plan something like this?

AMELIA. *(Fixes him in her gaze.)* What I want to know is, all those nights when you couldn't get to me fast enough — was at least part of that so this might happen? Were you trying to make it easier for this to happen?

JAMIE. *(Takes a gulp of air.)* But I want to marry you.

AMELIA. I got rid of it this morning. *(She stares evenly at him. For a long moment he is at an utter loss.)*

JAMIE. Oh, don't, please don't.

AMELIA. It's all gone. Nothing here anymore.

JAMIE. Poor Amelia.

AMELIA. I didn't say a word to you. I didn't think about you for a second. You didn't even know it was there, and now it's gone.

JAMIE. *(Recovering shockingly fast.)* You were terrified, and you thought you were all alone, but you're safe here, really you are, and this was just a test, that's all.

AMELIA. If this was a test then I've failed with flying colors.

48

JAMIE. Because you were right, you're always right, about everything, this wasn't the time yet for this.

AMELIA. It will never be the time.

JAMIE. But the only thing I want in this world is to look at your face. I just want to look at your face. *(He takes her face in his hands. She stares at him for a moment.)*

AMELIA. See, I've been sleeping with Winston.

JAMIE. *(A moment, then:)* You're lying.

AMELIA. Now tell me how much you want to look at my face.

JAMIE. I don't know why you're lying but you are.

AMELIA. We've been doing it for a month now.

JAMIE. You're just saying stuff now. You don't even know what you're saying.

AMELIA. Right here in your apartment, right under your nose, the moment your back was turned, every night when he was painting me.

JAMIE. What are you doing to me?

AMELIA. I think I'm in love with him. I'm in love with him.

JAMIE. This is all because of the goddamned painting. *(Jamie shoves the back of the easel. The canvas crashes to the floor. He bolts into the bedroom, shoving aside the hanging beads.)*

AMELIA. No, don't, just don't — *(Amelia starts after him. Without warning Winston flies backward through the beads, propelled as if shoved. Jamie is close behind. He winds up for a roundhouse punch. Winston backs away but Jamie still manages to catch him on the jaw. Winston trips and falls to the floor. Jamie stands over him. Amelia and Winston stare at Jamie, horrified. Suddenly Jamie bursts into laughter.)*

JAMIE. *I* did this, didn't I?

AMELIA. I'm sorry. *(His laughter growing, Jamie stares at Winston and then at Amelia. He wipes his hands across his face.)*

JAMIE. I've got to get out of here. *(Jamie turns and runs into the bedroom. Amelia stares after him, hand to her mouth, astounded by her own cruelty. Winston rolls over on his side and turns toward her.)*

WINSTON. You told him?

AMELIA. I couldn't lie to him. *(Winston rises to his knees and stares at Amelia.)*

WINSTON. I don't understand. You've been lying to him really effectively for the past month.

AMELIA. I was being really cruel.

WINSTON. And now you're being really kind?

AMELIA. Of course not.

WINSTON. Why did you rub his nose in it? Do you hate him that much?

AMELIA. You know I don't hate him.

WINSTON. Or maybe you just like tossing grenades around. You think it's really thrilling to watch things blow up.

AMELIA. No, I don't — I just — *(Winston hoists himself up off the floor. Amelia leans against the wall, utterly spent.)*

WINSTON. It would've been the easiest thing in the world just to stop returning his phone calls, you know, it's a big city, you could've disappeared without a trace.

AMELIA. That would've been an awful thing to do.

WINSTON. Jamie would've cried for a week but then he would've gotten over it, and we could all, you know, get back to our lives.

AMELIA. *(Her eyes widening.)* Get back to our lives?

WINSTON. I don't want to have to find a new roommate, I'm used to Jamie, I can work around him, and, you know, I hate meeting new people.

AMELIA. *(Deeply confused.)* But I — don't you — what have we been doing for the past month?

WINSTON. I've been just, you know, I've been painting you.

AMELIA. *(In shocked disbelief.)* We've been doing a lot more than that and you know it.

WINSTON. I'm not sure, I mean, what exactly are you referring to?

AMELIA. *(At a loss for a moment.)* First off, we sure have been *talking* a whole lot.

WINSTON. Of course we talked, why wouldn't we? We've been spending five hours together every night, we had to do something to relieve the tedium.

AMELIA. It was more than — I told you everything.

WINSTON. Yeah, well, frankly I'm not sure why you told me so much. To be honest I found it all a little embarrassing.

AMELIA. Are you actually going to make me remind you that we've been sleeping together?

WINSTON. *(Extremely awkward.)* Well, that was kind of an accident, wasn't it? I mean, I was sketching you, and you were so nervous, so I thought, you know, maybe it would be a good way to calm you down.

AMELIA. You thought it would calm me down?

WINSTON. *(Stuffs his hands in his pockets.)* And after that, you know, when I was painting you, it seemed like you still wanted to do it, you were kind of, um, desperate to do it, and I thought, boy, I really don't want to do this again, but I thought if I said that, maybe I'd hurt your feelings, or we'd fight about it, and I didn't want that, plus I really wanted to finish the painting, so I just, you know, I did it.

AMELIA. That was awfully … charitable of you.

WINSTON. *(Stares at the floor.)* I guess maybe I should've not done it in the first place, huh?

AMELIA. But I'm in love with you.

WINSTON. *(Taken aback a little.)* Oh. Gosh. Well. Hmm.

AMELIA. *(Very slowly.)* Do you even know that I'm real? *(Jamie passes through the hanging beads and grabs his jackets from the coatrack in the vestibule.)*

JAMIE. I'll be out of your hair in fifteen minutes tops.

WINSTON. Jamie, really, um, no, you don't have to — *(Jamie stares at the clothes in his arms. He cannot even bear to look at Winston and Amelia. There is no anger in him, just pain and sorrow.)*

JAMIE. I'll stay at Janelle's tonight, I'll come back for the rest of my stuff tomorrow. Or maybe I'll just leave everything here, let that be my gift to you.

AMELIA. We don't deserve any gifts.

JAMIE. *(Smiles fondly at them.)* Let me do you one favor after all this, let this be my one good deed, okay? *(Quickly Jamie disappears into the bedroom. Winston stares after him.)*

WINSTON. I should talk to him, right, I'll try and talk him down a little — *(Winston starts toward the bedroom. Desperately Amelia runs toward him and tackles him, pushing him down on to the mattress. Winston is flabbergasted.)*

AMELIA. Stop it stop it stop it —

WINSTON. What are you — I don't — *(Amelia lies on top of Winston on the floor, pounding her fists into his chest, sobbing uncontrollably.)*

AMELIA. Would it kill you to ask me about my day? Just to be pleasant. Just to be civil. And would it kill you to — would it kill you to —

WINSTON. I don't, I mean, I'm not. *(Amelia raises her arms. She wipes her teary face with the back of her hand. Utterly lost and mournful, she puts her hands on her belly.)*

AMELIA. Look, there's not even a trace of it left anymore. If I want to I can pretend it wasn't there to begin with. I don't even look any different, do I?

WINSTON. *(As gently as possible.)* You look the same to me. *(Amelia leans down very close to Winston and whispers into his ear.)*

AMELIA. You know I did this because of you. *(Instinctively Winston rises, shoving Amelia violently off him. He retreats to the wall, moving as far away from her as he can.)*

WINSTON. No! No! That's not — you were already going to do it, you would have done it anyway —

AMELIA. *(A howl of pain.)* No! The way it happened, I did it because of what we said to each other, I did it because of what we did, I did it because of you — !

WINSTON. *(Absolutely infuriated.)* Don't! Don't! I was completely up front with you, that I — that this sort of thing, you know, it doesn't happen for me, I'm not interested in it, I don't want it, really I'd just like to be left alone. Apparently you were hanging on my every word. How come all of that managed to slip by?

AMELIA. No, I heard you say it, I did.

WINSTON. And what? You thought it didn't apply to you? You thought you were the big exception?

AMELIA. *(A slow horror.)* Yeah, I guess that's what I thought.

WINSTON. Forgive me for saying so, but that was awfully conceited of you.

AMELIA. *(Quietly devastated.)* Then was this all in fun for you? Do you have so much contempt for me, you can do whatever you want to me and it doesn't matter?

WINSTON. I have nothing against you. *(They stare at each other across the width of the room. All of Amelia's other emotions burn away, and she considers him with naked pain.)*

AMELIA. Why do you so badly need to make me feel I was wrong about you?

WINSTON. *(Looks down, his voice low.)* This isn't me, this is all you.

AMELIA. Are you scared of how overwhelmed you can get when you let yourself? Is that what it is?

WINSTON. What happened was, you were afraid to leave Jamie and get rid of the baby. So you made up that I was in love with you, because it made you feel better to pretend that you were running *to* somebody instead of just running away.

AMELIA. I don't believe that. I don't. Is it because you feel awful about Jamie? Is that it?

WINSTON. I was just, I said, I was painting you.

AMELIA. Or do you hate Jamie? Did you just use me to get back at him?

WINSTON. You know that's not true.

AMELIA. Or maybe you want to fuck Jamie, and I'm the closest you could get.

WINSTON. Now you're just trying to be hateful.

AMELIA. *(At the end of her rope.)* You have me in the palm of your hand. If you close your fist around me now you'll crush me. I won't survive it. So I'm begging you — if any of this was real, even for a second — don't.

WINSTON. *(As simply as possible.)* Maybe I should've looked at you more closely, maybe then I would've seen what was happening, maybe then I could've stopped it. I just didn't see it. But everything you thought I saw in you — none of that was true, you made it all up.

AMELIA. So I did all of this, and none of it was real?

WINSTON. And this past month, you know, you've kept me from getting enough sleep, you've distracted me from my thesis, which I very much need to finish. And now you've caused a catastrophe from which it'll take me at least a month to recover. So at this point, you know, all I really wish is that you'd go.

AMELIA. *(Lets out a soft moan.)* Look at you: You don't even know what you've done.

WINSTON. If it would make you feel better to think that. *(A large bag is kicked through the beads. Jamie follows after it. Amelia turns to look at him. All of a sudden she throws open the front door and runs out of the apartment. The door slams shut. Jamie stares after her. Winston does not. Jamie moves to the kitchen cabinets.)* I don't want you to go.

JAMIE. These are my pots, right? I'll leave you this one, that way you can cook your ramen noodles tonight, okay?

WINSTON. *(Extends his arms hopelessly.)* Believe it or not, I was, um, just trying to help.

JAMIE. *(Stares at him, then, laughs.)* Awful truth, that probably *is* what you were trying to do. *(Jamie throws his bag over his shoulder. All of a sudden he collapses and puts his head in his hands, shaking violently. Winston does not know what to do. He kneels down and puts his hands on the sides of Jamie's head.)*

WINSTON. I'm, uh, really I'm, uh. *(Jamie looks up at Winston. They stare at each other, entangled in a ridiculous kind of embrace. Then Jamie starts to laugh.)*

JAMIE. So, what, now you want to help me some more? *(Winston takes his hands away and rises. He turns and disappears into the back room. Alone now, Jamie allows himself to cry. His howls are enormous and heaving and frightening. The lights fade.)*

Scene 2

It's nearly dusk on a Sunday in October, four years later. The beads hanging from the bedroom door are gone, and the back room is now filled with canvases. Otherwise the place hasn't changed much. If anything it's even more cluttered.

A woman stands with her back to us. She turns, and we discover that it is Amelia. She is dressed in a purple cashmere sweater and grey slacks. Heels. Lovely but not overly opulent jewelry. A tasteful amount of base and blush. Her hair is ornately pinned up.

She considers her surroundings very closely, as if she does not want to let any detail escape her notice.

Winston emerges from the bathroom holding a glass of water. He wears glasses now, but otherwise he looks entirely the same. He may even be wearing the exact same pair of paint-spattered sweatpants.

AMELIA. I forgot that you don't have a kitchen sink.

WINSTON. It's rustic living, but, um, I like it. *(He hands her the glass of water.)*

AMELIA. For the life of me I did not expect to find you here. I thought, I've got a couple hours before I have to catch the train back to Connecticut, I should visit all my old haunts. I saw your name on the buzzer, I nearly jumped out of my skin. I can't believe you're still living in this place.

WINSTON. I really hate, you know, moving. *(Attempting conviviality.)* So, what brings you to the city?

AMELIA. I spent the day uptown at the Jean-Paul Credeaux exhibit.

WINSTON. No kidding.

AMELIA. You've seen it, of course.

WINSTON. Yeah, um, a few months ago, when it opened.

AMELIA. What a madhouse. Lines around the block. Well, you predicted it. And it only took four years.

WINSTON. Four years? Really? Boy, time sure flies when you're, um, not paying attention.

AMELIA. And me, squeezing my way through the turnstiles, past the middle-aged couples from Passaic and the German families on holiday and the old ladies in their sensible shoes killing time before the matinee. I couldn't believe what a tourist I've become. I spent so many years trying to make this place my home, and now look at me, I am truly a stranger in this town.

WINSTON. *(A moment, then:)* I thought about calling you, you know, when Jamie died.

AMELIA. *(As neutral as possible.)* That would've been nice.

WINSTON. I wasn't even sure, um, you knew it had happened.

AMELIA. His stepmother wrote me. Remember her? Gail? A lovely note. I was awfully touched that she — I mean, I only met her once, I wasn't even aware that I had entered her mind. *(Looks down, her voice low.)* One thing I was sort of morbidly curious about, she didn't tell me *how* he — I don't know why, but that seems important to know.

WINSTON. *(Squirming a little.)* Oh. Well. He, uh, swallowed a bottle of pills. In a girl's apartment, on Chrystie Street, I think. I didn't get all the details, either.

AMELIA. You weren't in touch with him, then?

WINSTON. *(Shakes his head.)* I hadn't seen him in, what, six months at least. Actually the last day I saw him was, you know, the last day I saw you. *(A beat.)* I looked for you at the funeral.

AMELIA. *(Smiles sadly.)* I didn't hear about it in time. I don't think I could've gone anyway. It would've been kind of a travesty for me to be there, don't you think?

WINSTON. That's the reason I wanted to call you, um, I was really afraid you would take it on yourself, what happened to Jamie. But he had always been so unhappy, you know, his mom dying when he was so young, and then his dad and all, plus there was probably so much more going on that, um, we never even knew about.

AMELIA. *(Stares at him evenly.)* That's a comforting thing to say, but sometimes I wake up in the middle of the night in a cold sweat and I lie in the tub shivering till dawn, or I walk across the play-ground and I start shaking all over and I have to sit in my car till it passes. And then I have to admit that in the end he did it entirely because of me. It was you and me.

WINSTON. *(Deeply uncomfortable.)* So, um, what have you been doing with yourself in Connecticut?

AMELIA. Past three years I've been the chorus teacher at Ridgefield Elementary School.

WINSTON. Wow, um, that must be fun, I guess. And I noticed, um, a wedding ring.

AMELIA. Would you believe the gym teacher?

WINSTON. No way. Kids too?

AMELIA. *(Nods.)* Twins. Jack and Sarah. Gabe took them on an outing in the country today. A petting zoo. Which he's happy to do, because believe me, he'd rather swallow glass than waste his Sunday at a museum. Not even to look at paintings of naked ladies. I have photos of everybody in my wallet but I won't bore you.

WINSTON. No, um, I'd really like to see.

AMELIA. *(Flashes him a bright smile.)* Actually I'm not sure I want to show you anything.

WINSTON. *(A moment, then, raises his hands.)* Oh. Okay. Fine. Whatever. *(A pause.)* It seems like, um, you're really happy.

AMELIA. Oh, sure. I mean, there are moments, particularly

when they're getting especially cranky in their car seats, or when Gabe pitches a fit because I threw his favorite sweats in the laundry or something asinine like that. And then it's like I can *feel* the life draining out of me. But then I'm putting them to bed, and Gabe is dozing in front of the TV, and the house is so peaceful, and I have this tremendous sense of ... relief.

WINSTON. That sounds, you know, very nice.

AMELIA. And what about you? Is there anyone important in your life?

WINSTON. *(Stuffs his hands in his pockets.)* No. There's no one important in my life.

AMELIA. We get the Sunday *Times* so Gabe can do the crossword, I always flip through the Arts and Leisure section looking for your name.

WINSTON. Oh, well, that would be kind of, um, a fool's errand.

AMELIA. How have things been going? *(Distractedly Winston sharpens his pencils with his paring knife.)*

WINSTON. I cart my portfolio around. But everybody's pretty much already seen me. The consensus is my stuff is too remote and technical, it feels more like, um, an exercise than an expression, I'm too derivative and far too, you know, self-consciously imitative.

AMELIA. But you're still painting every day.

WINSTON. *(Extends his arms helplessly.)* What else am I going to do?

AMELIA. *(A moment, then, nods.)* Well. I admire your persistence.

WINSTON. There was one flurry of activity a while back. Do you remember that awful day — Tess Anderson Rose actually bought one of my paintings. When she died, Christie's auctioned off her entire collection. So there was a week when I got about a hundred phone calls from the auction house, I had to fax them my bio for the catalogue, it was all, you know, pretty entertaining.

AMELIA. Did your painting fetch a good price?

WINSTON. *(Shakes his head.)* They couldn't give it away. But the Jean-Paul Credeaux still life she owned, that went for three and a half million dollars.

AMELIA. I saw it in the exhibit. It's really a wonderful painting, isn't it? And the portraits of those prostitutes — my God! I didn't understand them when you showed me the pictures in the magazine, but to see them up close — those women! One of them is barely twelve years old, one of them, you can tell she's going to be dead within a week, but they're all just sitting there bathed in this extraordinary, thick kind of light.

WINSTON. I know, it's, um, amazing, isn't it?

AMELIA. But what really makes them masterpieces — it's how they're all looking at you so intensely. The way their eyes are lit up, it's like they could burn a hole in you. But of course what they were really looking at is *him*. They're staring at him with such joy and such *gratitude*, you can tell it's because in their entire lives nobody ever looked at them the way he's looking at them.

WINSTON. I never, you know, I never thought of it like that.

AMELIA. And you can tell that the way he's looking at them, it's with this tremendous kind of ... well, the only word for it is *love*. It's just a momentary love, and it's certainly a sick and twisted kind of love, but all the same ... it's so clear that he loved them.

WINSTON. *(Immediately flaring up.)* Look, don't you have a train to catch? Can I put you in a cab or something? Because I've got, you know, a lot of work to do, and frankly this whole conversation is just getting really annoying. I'm not even sure why you came here.

AMELIA. You know why I'm here. Do you still have it? *(He pulls out the easel from its resting place and sets it down under the skylight. He heads into the back room.)* Walking through those galleries, my heart was pounding so fast, every time I turned a corner I kept expecting to see my face. *(He strides back into the front room holding the canvas. He sets it down on the easel in front of her.)*

WINSTON. Upsettingly enough, this is, I think, the best thing I've ever done. *(He steps back toward the wall. She stares at the canvas. Her legs nearly give way beneath her. She bites her lip to keep from crying. She gets her water glass from the table and drinks it down in one gulp, her eyes on the painting. Winston rises and steps toward her.)* Would you like, um, another glass of water?

AMELIA. Thank you, I would. *(He takes the glass from her and retreats into the bathroom. Impulsively she goes to the table and picks up the paring knife. She takes the knife and shoves it toward the canvas as though about to slash it straight through. Winston comes out of the bathroom.)*

WINSTON. Go ahead. If you want. Please.

AMELIA. *(Turns to him.)* Why bother? It won't make me feel any better. And at least this way, there's one thing in this world that'll make you think about me.

WINSTON. *(Aching with regret.)* I am never not thinking about you. *(He lets out a sob. She stares at him for a moment. Then she puts down the knife. She gestures toward the canvas.)*

AMELIA. Please: Explain for me what you did here.

WINSTON. It wasn't me. It's all, um, Credeaux. I was just faking it.

AMELIA. Tell me what you were faking, then. *(He hesitates, then takes a few steps toward the easel. He extends his arms toward the canvas.)*

WINSTON. You proceed as if you're afraid you're about to run out of paint. The end effect being that every gesture is essential, nothing is squandered.

AMELIA. I can see that now.

WINSTON. And with the woman — you try to capture all her contradictory aspects. The way her body is both exposed and concealed, how she's both ashamed and thrilled to be naked. *(She gazes at the painting with such intensity that it seems as though she might burn a hole in it.)* And you enhance this in the face: The orange slit of the smile, the flecks of topaz for her eyes — she looks out at you with such fire and such love — you could spend the rest of your life swallowed up in her gaze.

AMELIA. You're right: That's what was there.

WINSTON. But the most important thing is the moon, the way it starts as a tiny peal of light but then it gradually bathes the room, the way it seems like all you have to do is paint the light around her and then you'll discover her inside of it, reaching out for you.

AMELIA. She puts me to shame. *(He stares at her. Her eyes are locked on the canvas.)*

End of Play

PROPERTY LIST

Box of cereal (WINSTON)
Art book (WINSTON)
Books, papers (WINSTON)
Magazine (WINSTON)
Paints, brushes (WINSTON)
Wristwatch (AMELIA)
2 large shopping bags with food inside: muffins, croissants,
    scones, coffees, juice carton (JAMIE)
Jeans (WINSTON)
2 glasses (JAMIE)
Vodka (JAMIE)
Glass (WINSTON, AMELIA)
Paring knife, pencils (WINSTON)
Blanket, sketchpad (WINSTON)
Bottle of Maker's Mark (AMELIA)
Glass of water (WINSTON)
Handbag (TESS)
Small painting (WINSTON)
Painting (JAMIE)
Checkbook, pen (TESS)
Large bag (JAMIE)

NEW PLAYS

★ **YELLOW FACE by David Henry Hwang.** Asian-American playwright DHH leads a protest against the casting of Jonathan Pryce as the Eurasian pimp in the original Broadway production of *Miss Saigon*, condemning the practice as "yellowface." The lines between truth and fiction blur with hilarious and moving results in this unreliable memoir. "A pungent play of ideas with a big heart." —*Variety.* "Fabulously inventive." —*The New Yorker.* [5M, 2W] ISBN: 978-0-8222-2301-6

★ **33 VARIATIONS by Moisés Kaufmann.** A mother coming to terms with her daughter. A composer coming to terms with his genius. And, even though they're separated by 200 years, these two people share an obsession that might, even just for a moment, make time stand still. "A compellingly original and thoroughly watchable play for today." —*Talkin' Broadway.* [4M, 4W] ISBN: 978-0-8222-2392-4

★ **BOOM by Peter Sinn Nachtrieb.** A grad student's online personal ad lures a mysterious journalism student to his subterranean research lab. But when a major catastrophic event strikes the planet, their date takes on evolutionary significance and the fate of humanity hangs in the balance. "Darkly funny dialogue." —*NY Times.* "Literate, coarse, thoughtful, sweet, scabrously inappropriate." —*Washington City Paper.* [1M, 2W] ISBN: 978-0-8222-2370-2

★ **LOVE, LOSS AND WHAT I WORE by Nora Ephron and Delia Ephron, based on the book by Ilene Beckerman.** A play of monologues and ensemble pieces about women, clothes and memory covering all the important subjects—mothers, prom dresses, mothers, buying bras, mothers, hating purses and why we only wear black. "Funny, compelling." —*NY Times.* "So funny and so powerful." —*WowOwow.com.* [5W] ISBN: 978-0-8222-2355-9

★ **CIRCLE MIRROR TRANSFORMATION by Annie Baker.** When four lost New Englanders enrolled in Marty's community center drama class experiment with harmless games, hearts are quietly torn apart, and tiny wars of epic proportions are waged and won. "Absorbing, unblinking and sharply funny." —*NY Times.* [2M, 3W] ISBN: 978-0-8222-2445-7

★ **BROKE-OLOGY by Nathan Louis Jackson.** The King family has weathered the hardships of life and survived with their love for each other intact. But when two brothers are called home to take care of their father, they find themselves strangely at odds. "Engaging dialogue." —*TheaterMania.com.* "Assured, bighearted." —*Time Out.* [3M, 1W] ISBN: 978-0-8222-2428-0

DRAMATISTS PLAY SERVICE, INC.
440 Park Avenue South, New York, NY 10016 212-683-8960 Fax 212-213-1539
postmaster@dramatists.com www.dramatists.com

NEW PLAYS

★ **A CIVIL WAR CHRISTMAS: AN AMERICAN MUSICAL CELEBRATION by Paula Vogel, music by Daryl Waters.** It's 1864, and Washington, D.C. is settling down to the coldest Christmas Eve in years. Intertwining many lives, this musical shows us that the gladness of one's heart is the best gift of all. "Boldly inventive theater, warm and affecting." *–Talkin' Broadway.* "Crisp strokes of dialogue." *–NY Times.* [12M, 5W] ISBN: 978-0-8222-2361-0

★ **SPEECH & DEBATE by Stephen Karam.** Three teenage misfits in Salem, Oregon discover they are linked by a sex scandal that's rocked their town. "Savvy comedy." *–Variety.* "Hilarious, cliché-free, and immensely entertaining." *–NY Times.* "A strong, rangy play." *–NY Newsday.* [2M, 2W] ISBN: 978-0-8222-2286-6

★ **DIVIDING THE ESTATE by Horton Foote.** Matriarch Stella Gordon is determined not to divide her 100-year-old Texas estate, despite her family's declining wealth and the looming financial crisis. But her three children have another plan. "Goes for laughs and succeeds." *–NY Daily News.* "The theatrical equivalent of a page-turner." *–Bloomberg.com.* [4M, 9W] ISBN: 978-0-8222-2398-6

★ **WHY TORTURE IS WRONG, AND THE PEOPLE WHO LOVE THEM by Christopher Durang.** Christopher Durang turns political humor upside down with this raucous and provocative satire about America's growing homeland "insecurity." "A smashing new play." *–NY Observer.* "You may laugh yourself silly." *–Bloomberg News.* [4M, 3W] ISBN: 978-0-8222-2401-3

★ **FIFTY WORDS by Michael Weller.** While their nine-year-old son is away for the night on his first sleepover, Adam and Jan have an evening alone together, beginning a suspenseful nightlong roller-coaster ride of revelation, rancor, passion and humor. "Mr. Weller is a bold and productive dramatist." *–NY Times.* [1M, 1W] ISBN: 978-0-8222-2348-1

★ **BECKY'S NEW CAR by Steven Dietz.** Becky Foster is caught in middle age, middle management and in a middling marriage—with no prospects for change on the horizon. Then one night a socially inept and grief-struck millionaire stumbles into the car dealership where Becky works. "Gently and consistently funny." *–Variety.* "Perfect blend of hilarious comedy and substantial weight." *–Broadway Hour.* [4M, 3W] ISBN: 978-0-8222-2393-1

DRAMATISTS PLAY SERVICE, INC.
440 Park Avenue South, New York, NY 10016 212-683-8960 Fax 212-213-1539
postmaster@dramatists.com www.dramatists.com

NEW PLAYS

★ **AT HOME AT THE ZOO by Edward Albee.** Edward Albee delves deeper into his play THE ZOO STORY by adding a first act, HOMELIFE, which precedes Peter's fateful meeting with Jerry on a park bench in Central Park. "An essential and heartening experience." *–NY Times.* "Darkly comic and thrilling." *–Time Out.* "Genuinely fascinating." *–Journal News.* [2M, 1W] ISBN: 978-0-8222-2317-7

★ **PASSING STRANGE book and lyrics by Stew, music by Stew and Heidi Rodewald, created in collaboration with Annie Dorsen.** A daring musical about a young bohemian that takes you from black middle-class America to Amsterdam, Berlin and beyond on a journey towards personal and artistic authenticity. "Fresh, exuberant, bracingly inventive, bitingly funny, and full of heart." *–NY Times.* "The freshest musical in town!" *–Wall Street Journal.* "Excellent songs and a vulnerable heart." *–Variety.* [4M, 3W] ISBN: 978-0-8222-2400-6

★ **REASONS TO BE PRETTY by Neil LaBute.** Greg really, truly adores his girlfriend, Steph. Unfortunately, he also thinks she has a few physical imperfections, and when he mentions them, all hell breaks loose. "Tight, tense and emotionally true." *–Time Magazine.* "Lively and compulsively watchable." *–The Record.* [2M, 2W] ISBN: 978-0-8222-2394-8

★ **OPUS by Michael Hollinger.** With only a few days to rehearse a grueling Beethoven masterpiece, a world-class string quartet struggles to prepare their highest-profile performance ever—a televised ceremony at the White House. "Intimate, intense and profoundly moving." *–Time Out.* "Worthy of scores of bravissimos." *–BroadwayWorld.com.* [4M, 1W] ISBN: 978-0-8222-2363-4

★ **BECKY SHAW by Gina Gionfriddo.** When an evening calculated to bring happiness takes a dark turn, crisis and comedy ensue in this wickedly funny play that asks what we owe the people we love and the strangers who land on our doorstep. "As engrossing as it is ferociously funny." *–NY Times.* "Gionfriddo is some kind of genius." *–Variety.* [2M, 3W] ISBN: 978-0-8222-2402-0

★ **KICKING A DEAD HORSE by Sam Shepard.** Hobart Struther's horse has just dropped dead. In an eighty-minute monologue, he discusses what path brought him here in the first place, the fate of his marriage, his career, politics and eventually the nature of the universe. "Deeply instinctual and intuitive." *–NY Times.* "The brilliance is in the infinite reverberations Shepard extracts from his simple metaphor." *–TheaterMania.* [1M, 1W] ISBN: 978-0-8222-2336-8

DRAMATISTS PLAY SERVICE, INC.
440 Park Avenue South, New York, NY 10016 212-683-8960 Fax 212-213-1539
postmaster@dramatists.com www.dramatists.com

NEW PLAYS

★ **AUGUST: OSAGE COUNTY by Tracy Letts.** WINNER OF THE 2008 PULITZER PRIZE AND TONY AWARD. When the large Weston family reunites after Dad disappears, their Oklahoma homestead explodes in a maelstrom of repressed truths and unsettling secrets. "Fiercely funny and bitingly sad." *–NY Times.* "Ferociously entertaining." *–Variety.* "A hugely ambitious, highly combustible saga." *–NY Daily News.* [6M, 7W] ISBN: 978-0-8222-2300-9

★ **RUINED by Lynn Nottage.** WINNER OF THE 2009 PULITZER PRIZE. Set in a small mining town in Democratic Republic of Congo, RUINED is a haunting, probing work about the resilience of the human spirit during times of war. "A full-immersion drama of shocking complexity and moral ambiguity." *–Variety.* "Sincere, passionate, courageous." *–Chicago Tribune.* [8M, 4W] ISBN: 978-0-8222-2390-0

★ **GOD OF CARNAGE by Yasmina Reza, translated by Christopher Hampton.** WINNER OF THE 2009 TONY AWARD. A playground altercation between boys brings together their Brooklyn parents, leaving the couples in tatters as the rum flows and tensions explode. "Satisfyingly primitive entertainment." *–NY Times.* "Elegant, acerbic, entertainingly fueled on pure bile." *–Variety.* [2M, 2W] ISBN: 978-0-8222-2399-3

★ **THE SEAFARER by Conor McPherson.** Sharky has returned to Dublin to look after his irascible, aging brother. Old drinking buddies Ivan and Nicky are holed up at the house too, hoping to play some cards. But with the arrival of a stranger from the distant past, the stakes are raised ever higher. "Dark and enthralling Christmas fable." *–NY Times.* "A timeless classic." *–Hollywood Reporter.* [5M] ISBN: 978-0-8222-2284-2

★ **THE NEW CENTURY by Paul Rudnick.** When the playwright is Paul Rudnick, expectations are geared for a play both hilarious and smart, and this provocative and outrageous comedy is no exception. "The one-liners fly like rockets." *–NY Times.* "The funniest playwright around." *–Journal News.* [2M, 3W] ISBN: 978-0-8222-2315-3

★ **SHIPWRECKED! AN ENTERTAINMENT—THE AMAZING ADVENTURES OF LOUIS DE ROUGEMONT (AS TOLD BY HIMSELF) by Donald Margulies.** The amazing story of bravery, survival and celebrity that left nineteenth-century England spellbound. Dare to be whisked away. "A deft, literate narrative." *–LA Times.* "Springs to life like a theatrical pop-up book." *–NY Times.* [2M, 1W] ISBN: 978-0-8222-2341-2

DRAMATISTS PLAY SERVICE, INC.
440 Park Avenue South, New York, NY 10016 212-683-8960 Fax 212-213-1539
postmaster@dramatists.com www.dramatists.com